Anarchism & Environmental Survival

by

Graham Purchase

See Sharp Press ◆ Tucson, Arizona ◆ 1994

For information contact See Sharp Press, P.O. Box 1731,
Tucson, AZ 85702-1731.

Purchase, Graham.
    Anarchism & environmental survival / by Graham
Purchase ; introduction by Chaz Bufe. – Tucson, AZ : See Sharp
Press, 1993.
    160 p. ; 23 cm.
    Includes bibliographical references.

1. Human ecology. 2. Land use – Environmental aspects.
3. Environmental policy. 4. Green movement. 5. Anarchism.
6. Agricultural ecology.

ISBN: 0-9613289-8-3   304.28

First Printing

Cover graphics by Clifford Harper. Cover and interior design by Chaz Bufe.
Interior text typeset in 11-point Baskerville. Cover typeset in Optima.
Printed on acid-free paper with soy-based ink by Thomson-Shore, Inc.,
Dexter, Michigan.

Contents

Introduction

One of the most consistently levelled and damaging criticisms of anarchists is that they lack a positive vision of the future. A more sophisticated and perhaps even more damaging criticism is that anarchists' visions of a free and egalitarian society are hopelessly utopian—that they have no idea of "how to get from here to there." Unfortunately, many anarchists have done nothing to counter these criticisms, and some have actually made the situation worse by their insistence that anarchism is an anti-organizational and/or anti-programmatic ideology. This is far from the truth, as a brief look at the writings of the most outstanding anarchist theorists—Rudolf Rocker, Peter Kropotkin, Errico Malatesta, Murray Bookchin, et al.—will show. But these damaging and enduring myths continue to mar anarchism's reputation.

A contributing factor to the endurance of these myths is the fact that anarchists have produced remarkably few works over the last half century outlining *positive* visions of an anarchist society. Thus, I'm very happy that See Sharp Press is publishing this much-needed book in which Graham Purchase outlines a radically positive, achievable vision of an ecologically integrated anarchist society; just as importantly, he provides us with a number of practical steps necessary to the realization that vision.

In the following essays, Graham deals with virtually every important issue on the anarchist and Green agendas: bio-regionalism; technology and its effects on the environment; population; the organization of work; feminism and its relationship to both anarchism and environmentalism; chaos theory and its relation to anarchist theory; animal rights and vegetarianism; and the social ecology of Murray Bookchin. In dealing with these matters, Graham presents an anarchist vision which seems eminently *practical*—and so I believe that this book is an important step forward in convincing our fellow citizens that what Graham terms eco-anarchism is a reasonable and desirable alternative to the authoritarianism and environmental degradation which permeate so many aspects of daily life.

It should be emphasized, however, that in this book Graham Purchase is outlining one possible way in which society might be reorganized along eco-anarchist lines. It should also be emphasized that Graham is not advocating a quick fix; if society were to choose the path he outlines, eco-social reorganization would not be an overnight process. Even in the rosiest scenario, it would take decades to undo the social damage wrought by industrial capitalism and "communism," and perhaps centuries to undo the environmental damage.

As well, Graham is *not* arguing that his vision should be imposed upon the rest of us; rather, he is offering his vision in the hope that it will serve as a road map for the *voluntary* reorganization of society—or, at the least, will stimulate others to reconsider their own desires about the type of society in which they wish to live, and to work toward the realization of their desires.

—Chaz Bufe, April 25, 1994

Preface

As a result of the environmental crisis, the once-unshakable belief that the human species should dominate nature is being challenged on all sides. "Survival" has come to mean something more complex than the simplistic notion of "survival of the fittest" or the right of dominance by a "superior" species. Increasing numbers of people are coming to see that regional and planetary environmental health, and human survival itself, depend upon a respectful approach to nature and to non-human life forms. We now know that healthy soils, animals, forests, grasslands and river systems are biological necessities for human survival. Ecological science further tells us that genetic and species *diversity*, not homogeneity, ensures the health and stability of ecosystems, and that the health and stability of the Earth itself can be no greater than that of its combined ecological regions. Our contemporary understanding of survival, then, and the means necessary to its realization, is a far cry from the individualistic struggle for existence—"Nature red in tooth and claw"—once depicted in elementary biology texts. Human survival depends not upon competition with other species (and within our own), but rather upon the adoption of cooperative and nurturant ways of life—a sustainable course of co-evolution with all living things.

At the same time, people are increasingly looking for non-governmental ways to solve pressing social and environmental problems. They realize that it is everyone's responsibility to create a greener, healthier, and more sustainable future for their families and communities. People are beginning to plant trees in suburban "green belts," to campaign against the pollution of local rivers, and to take the time to appreciate the wildlife in their regions. They notice that the massive and imperialistic military and economic ventures of nation states and multinational corporations are more often than not harmful to the regions in which they are imposed. Corporate capitalism, from Tokyo to Berlin, seems determined to cover the delicate ecoregions of our living planet with a universal landscape of asphalt highways, golf courses, shopping malls, and theme parks. People everywhere are realizing that our survival is dependent upon environmental stability, and that the pathological interests of governments and multinational corporations pose the single biggest threat to the health of the Earth.

Despite the media's ignorant but never-ending attempts to depict anarchy as synonymous with chaos and disorder, it is becoming clearer every day that something new must replace the outmoded philosophy of deathly order, greed and destruction. Anarchy—literally, simply "no state" or "without a state"—calls for the replacememt of the state and capitalism by federations of economically cooperating, ecoregionally integrated communities. Today, anarchism is emerging as the only credible philosophy of survival—whether it's called "anarchism" or not. Since the collapse of the French Revolution (1789–1793) two centuries ago, when the first true representatives of anarchy (the *enrages*) did battle with the forces of clergy, aristocracy and capital, there has been an almost unending campaign to slur and misrepresent the ideas and practices of the organized anarchist movement. When cities or countries are in a state of turmoil and dislocation due to political struggles, economic failure, or national calamity, the journalist never fails to inform the public that "the situation has degenerated into anarchy!" (In fact, the idea that anarchy means disorder and chaos has become so entrenched that it is so defined in the *Oxford English Dictionary*!) For this reason, many people who understand what anarchism really stands for often reproach us for not changing the name of our movement to something that is not so frightening. But for more than a century, libertarians have called in the name of anarchy for a society that is decentralized and Green. Many thousands of people have lost their lives fighting for the cause of anarchism, and it would be unthinkable not to honor our intellectual ancestors who wrote, worked, or were martyred under anarchy's black banner.

In the 19th and early 20th centuries, Russian, American, Spanish, French, and Italian anarchists were exiled, imprisoned and executed by the thousands merely for expressing their opinions. Sadly, such persecution continues in many countries today; but in most, our ideas, publications, and bookshops are at least tolerated, if officially ignored and routinely slandered. It seems as if all movements pursuing genuine and lasting change must go through this process, with social disapproval gradually and grudgingly giving way to acceptance. After all, an idea or a movement that cannot survive at least a few centuries of persecution is in all probability not worth the bother. Anarchism has survived, and survives still.

A century ago, political theory was relatively simple, and the meanings of the terms "socialist," "anarchist," and "communist" were reasonably unambiguous. With the expansion of the university system after World War II, though, a whole host of new political divisions and sub-divisions has arisen—seemingly dreamed up overnight by trendy academics anxious to secure a niche for themselves and a brand name under which to sell their wares in university and "progressive" bookstores.

In the 1970s we had Marxist-Leninists, Socialist-Feminists, Anarchist-Feminists, etc.; but with the decline of Marxism's appeal and the rise of ecology, the 1980s saw a whole new range of "isms" and "ologies": Social Ecology, Deep Ecology, and Ecofeminism, for example. University lecturers have produced hundreds of articles on the Deep Ecology/Social Ecology debate alone, and as the 1990s progress we can expect a further fragmentation of intellectual thought into an ever-greater array of purportedly opposing positions. Indeed, such controversies form the ideal subject matter for the standard academic article, which usually compares two or three positions on a certain subject, and discusses their various histories, strengths, and weaknesses, typically without offering anything new or creative. Thus, the social, political, and ecological debate has degenerated into an overly dramatic and inward-looking quagmire of "isms" and "ologies"—many of which borrow ideas from anarchism.

Deep Ecology (the biological equality of all living things), Social Ecology (the ecoregionally integrated community as opposed to capitalist individualism and the nation state), and Ecofeminism (the need to repair the social and environmental damage resulting from patriarchal attitudes and structures) are all inherent in anarchist philosophy. My message to the proponents of all of them is, "forget your intellectual egotism and declare openly that you are all (among other things) anarchists!" You should be proud to contribute to a movement that has for two centuries opposed capitalism, patriarchy, institutional hierarchy, and arbitrary power, advocating instead human-scaled, self-administered, and ecologically integrated communities reliant upon low-impact food, waste, transportation, and energy technologies, and envisioning a global federation of free communities. My wish is to see the various groups come together and acknowledge that no good whatsoever can come from the fragmentation of a unified body of social, political, and ethical thinking into ever-diversifying, specialized "isms." Insofar as each hopes to achieve an ecologically integrated society in the absence of government, capitalism, and hierarchy, Deep Ecology, Social Ecology, and Ecofeminism want the same thing. The differences between these new philosophies are like petals on the bud of one flower, whose blooming will coincide with global harmony and the realization of the social and ecological revolution.

What the present power elite calls order is but one form of social order (hierarchy), and it's a type which causes a great deal of environmental *dis*order. Far from advocating disorder, anarchists argue for a new kind of order rooted in the natural ecoregional organization of life on Earth. In place of the nation state, anarchists argue that the organization of space and place should be based upon the natural geographical region. In place of centralized government, anarchists argue that the primary unit of economic, social and political life should be the self-governing, self-sufficient, and ecoregionally integrated village, town or city. In place of agribusiness, anarchists argue for a local, small-scale, permacultural approach to food production. In place of industrial capitalism, anarchists argue for the production of socially necessary goods and services using environmentally integrated technologies—organized by workers for the benefit of themselves and of humanity, rather than for a ruling class of parasites and environmental hooligans. This is the real "new world order," one which anarchists have been advocating for generations.

And how has the press labeled the anarchist vision? "Chaos!" "Disorder!" By implication, "order" is represented by the status quo: nine-tenths of humanity in poverty while a tiny minority squander the Earth's resources. "Order" is the degradation of America's agricultural lands through the monocultural pro- duction of wheat and cattle for the profit of powerful corporate elites. It is the despoliation of countless ecological regions and ecosystems by multinational corporations and their government lackeys. This, we are told, is good organization; and what is termed "disorder" often refers to rebellion—in the name of personal and environmental survival.

As the Green r/evolution grows apace with anarchism, there is a good chance that our doctrines will not merely survive, but will flourish. The essays that follow illustrate and elaborate upon this emerging synthesis of politics-not-as-usual and ecology.

The Community
and the Ecological Region

Life on Earth exists in a host of distinct ecological regions, roughly distinguished from one another by differences in topography, climate, drainage, and species distribution. In some places ecological regions are framed by physical features such as mountain ranges and sea coasts; in others, regional borders are less distinct. But we are so accustomed to seeing the world as "naturally" divided into nation states that we have forgotten that national borders are artificial creations that are often unrelated to geographical boundaries. Even within nations, land is parceled up in political, corporate, and individual units that ignore natural features. For example, a straight line between two Arab states cuts across the middle of a unique, well-defined desert; likewise, a charming river valley becomes unrecognizable after being divided into suburban blocks.

One task facing the emerging anarcho-environmental movement is to reverse this trend—to abolish the nation state and to foster in its place the ecoregional community. Eco-anarchists argue that the best way to preserve the health of the Earth is to restore the integrity of its parts, and that this depends on individuals acknowledging, nurturing, and protecting their home places.

People are starting to look to the past for answers. Through talking with their grandparents or looking at old photographs, both urban and rural people are realizing how much has been lost and are anxious to preserve what remains. The knowledge that a barren and degraded block of farmland was once an oak grove, or that a local river once teemed with cod or salmon, becomes a source of both sadness and inspiration as people become conscious of the need to restore their local regions.

Ultimately, only local residents will have the knowledge necessary to accomplish this enormous task of ecoregional revitalization.

If we are to reintegrate humanity with nature, it is critical that we first dismantle the nation state, which ignores ecological regions, and instead allow communities to reconstruct social, political and economic life based upon local environmental exigencies. This would eliminate both corporate interference and bureaucratic dictates from distant political bodies.

Social anarchists argue that, in the absence of the nation state, the free and ecoregionally integrated *commune* (or, in more modern terms, *community*) will again become the primary unit of social identification. The idea of the commune stems from revolutions in medieval Europe and 19th-century France, when the people in many cities attempted to regain political independence, first from the aristocracy and later from the bureaucratic and bourgeois classes. While French communes ranged from small hamlets to the mighty Paris Commune, they were all based on the belief that individuals' political identification should be with the autonomous village, town, city, or ecological region (or some combination thereof).

This general prescription, of course, says little about the actual nature of communities in the coming r/evolution. For example, will they be large or small? Does the integration of human social, economic and political life with the needs of the ecoregion necessarily imply the elimination of the city? Will property, labor and reward be distributed collectively or individually? Because these questions are the subject of intense debate in both the environmental and anarchist movements, we pause here to examine some of the major viewpoints and areas of emerging consensus.

One result of nationalism is that citizens have stopped thinking of cities as independent, living entities. In a world where power radiates from capitals in London, Paris and Tokyo, these potentially vibrant concentrations of human activity—villages, towns, and cities—have become mere symbols on a map. No longer an independent community, the small town has been figuratively reduced to an insignificant sucker on the tentacles of the national infrastructure. At the other end of the scale, the large cities—fueled by real estate greed and ill-conceived government "urban development plans"—have swollen to dozens if not hundreds of times their original size, after two centuries of migration from countrysides ravaged by deforestation and agribusiness despoliation. They have become little more than amorphous expanses of grey urban biomass. A crisis in ecoregional quality has accompanied this crisis in civic quality, with the blanketing of entire ecological regions in concrete and asphalt. Importing incredible amountss of water, energy, and food, and spewing out like amounts of garbage and waste into the surrounding countryside, the modern city is no longer a community but a doomed, human-dominated ecosystem which stands little or no chance of long-term survival.

The problems of large cities are of central concern to anarchists and to the newly emerging Green City movement. Both movements agree on four things: 1) if the present trend toward urban drift continues, in a few years—for the first time in history—the vast majority of people on Earth will live in cities; 2) the city is a natural product of a numerically successful, intensely social primate species whose members have diverse intellectual, economic and social needs; 3) given that humans appear to prefer living in cities, it is unrealistic to pretend that humanity will, at least in the short run, return to an exclusively small-scale, village-type existence; and 4) given the above, every effort should be made to make cities as self-sufficient as possible in water, energy, and food, and better integrated with the ecology of their surrounding regions. Cities are here, a given that we inherited from our forebears, and we have no choice but to deal with them as they are.

We must, however, reject one concept embraced by some Green City proponents—the high-tech Dome City idea, which owes more to science fiction novels and space movies than to reality. Using expanding biotechnologies, it would, for example, allow people to harvest "natural" wool in artificial growing mediums, and produce bio-fuels through botano-chemical processes, and create highly sophisticated air, water and waste recycling systems. Sealed in gigantic, transparent domes, such cities would be self-contained, self-sustaining ecosystems, taking in nothing from the outside and emitting nothing in return.

Scattered across the globe, these densely concentrated life-support systems would hypothetically allow the rest of nature to return to wilderness while humanity continued to evolve in spendid isolation. Recent pilot experiments in America, such as Arizona's Biosphere 2, show us that certain business interests are determined to realize the Dome City concept, and that this science fiction fantasy could indeed become a reality. The Japanese-backed Multi-Function Polis—a "high tech" city of 100,000 people to be built near Adelaide, Australia—is another dubious experiment, though still in the planning stage.

While sealed cities are perhaps suitable for colonizing lifeless, otherwise uninhabitable places like the moon, their presence in Earth's delicate environment—where everything must return to the Earth for good or for ill—would at best only delay eco-degradation. And people would not likely enjoy living in them; being part of some huge bio-machine is the stuff of nightmares, not of freedom and dignity. Humankind is part of nature and cannot be isolated from it; without nature in our daily lives, we would become like shriveled leaves stripped from a tree.

Apart from the Dome City concept, however, the idea of a self-sufficient and autonomous "Green City" is practicable. Local energy sources and urban horticulture, for example, are already practicable but foolishly underutilized and underfunded. Times are undoubtedly changing, though, as innovators discover new ways to recycle urban wastes and develop small-scale horticultural techniques that could transform the modern megalopolis. Low-head hydro power, poultry feeding from composted scraps, and wastewater aquaculture all represent existing "Green City" alternatives. Social anarchists foresee an expansion of such activities; we foresee that even inhabitants of city centers will one day eat vegetables and use electricity produced from the resources and waste of their own metropolises.

The anarchist-environmental r/evolution implies much more than a mere transfer of political power from one group of people to another. It requires, rather, an all-encompassing mini-revolution in every city, suburb, town, and village. Even after the political liberation of all these communities is achieved—probably through a general strike following a long period of educational and agitational work—the more important task of deconstructing and reconstructing daily life according to communally and environmentally sound principles will remain. This implies that each district must conduct its own r/evolution and apply the ideas of eco-anarchism to itself. Rather than relying on business or government to supply its basic needs, each community will rely on itself. This will happen in any case because, in the absence of law and authority, people will have to band together to prevent and punish crime. Communities will necessarily organize to provide utilities, mass transit, daycare, and a host of other activities necessary to human life.

(Imagine for a moment a rejuvenated metropolis, consisting of independent but federated suburban communities separated from one another by small groves of trees. All but the most necessary roads and fences have been removed and replaced by gardens, parks, fish ponds, and small-scale recycling plants; bicycle pathways and light rail networks connect the city's suburban communities. This city does not try to isolate itself from nature by covering everything with asphalt; rather, it integrates itself as closely as possible into the ecology of the surrounding region.)

The Green City concept is not, though, central to the anarchist blueprint for achieving global environmental harmony; in the future, anarchists might decide that cities are essentially anti-ecological in nature. However, faced as we are with cities of 20 to 30 million people (such as Tokyo and Mexico City), we must begin by changing our cities—the places in which most people will shortly live. These monstrous creations of state capitalism's centralist culture will, one hopes, "wither away" with the breakdown of centralization.

In re-creating the modern city, anarchists look to the pre-industrial city, such as the Greek and Sumerian city-state and the medieval European city-commune. We look to a period when cities were small enough to allow all their citizens to participate in important decisions, but large enough to supply a cosmopolitan alternative to village life. At present, though, this cultural reason for rural depopulation and city expansion has run full circle: life in the monotonous, faceless suburbs of the modern megalopolis is probably at least as boring as that in a sleepy 12th-century village. Luckily, the development of fast and efficient communication systems means that small-community lifestyles no longer necessitate the cultural isolation of previous eras.

In areas with very fragile environments, it may well be that small-village, isolated, and even nomadic lifestyles may be the most appropriate ways of human life. The existence of at least two million villages in the world today is evidence that the rural community is still viable. The self-sufficient Green City is not intended to supplant villages, but rather to take the pressure off rural areas and to make the city more livable. If the city could become self-sufficient in the production of food and most other necessities, it would allow rural people to concentrate on activities other than monocultural food production. Freed from the monotony of bulk food production, the rural population would have more time to devote to restoring and enhancing the seriously degraded soil. In addition, by easing pressure upon surrounding areas, a less dependent city would help save the remaining pockets of wilderness. This is important in that the wilderness has provided the raw material for "civilization," and it is still the only repository of the genetically variable wild "seed bank" necessary for true environmental reconstruction.

Unfortunately, since the industrial revolution, rural life in the West has become as endangered as the few remaining pockets of wilderness. In England, the rural economy has almost completely broken down; the nouveau riche have bought up the quaint cottages that the locals can no longer afford. Having run out of "bargains" close to London, the rich are busily buying abandoned farms and cottages across the channel in Brittany and Normandy. Meanwhile, in villages of countries like Greece and France, only the great grandmothers remain—their children and children's children having left long ago for Athens or Paris.

Social anarchists hope that the development of urban-agrarian environments within the shell of the decaying megalopolis will eliminate (or at least diminish) the arrogance that city dwellers often feel toward rural people. People in the city will, one hopes, learn to re-value the experience of "eating fresh strawberries while watching chickens fossicking at dawn"—not as part of a "country holiday package," but as part of everyday urban life.

But what of the idea of starting completely anew, of intentional rural communities? Since the advent of civilization, people have founded alternative communities in the wilderness, far away from the corrupting influences of the city. Such communities certainly existed in ancient Greece; likewise, medieval Christians attempted in much the same way to create the "pure Christian life" in the splendid isolation of the monastery. The deeply felt need to create a "new world" was the source of the "pioneer spirit" in the U.S. and Canada (never mind the dismal results of this "spirit"). Similarly, in the 18th and 19th centuries numerous political and religious groups, including the Russian Nihilists and some European anarchists, attempted to create "ideal communities" in remote areas of Siberia, Latin America, and rural Europe. The vast majority of these experiments failed rather quickly, and most of those that survived did so because they allowed themselves to become completely dominated by a single individual, whose charismatic personality kept dissent to a minimum.

Adherence to a particular social and political vision is not in itself a viable basis upon which to build a lasting community. Thus, although some of the more successful small-scale "intentional" communities later grew into small towns or cities (e.g., Saskatoon, in central Canada, founded as a temperance colony), these towns soon became much the same as other towns, with little or no awareness of the original philosophical, political or religious reasons which motivated their founding. Even when communities such as the Mennonites and Dukhobors in Canada succeeded in perpetuating their identity, they remained isolated in self-contained rural communities, and can hardly be said to have significantly influenced the wider society.

In modern times, the hippie experiments of the 1960s were inspired by a vision of free and ecologically integrated communities outside mainstream society. Again, many of these rural and wilderness communities failed due to isolation, internal disagreement, disorganization, lack of money, bad luck, or combinations thereof. The few that survived have typically done so by replacing their original practices of communal pooling of land and other resources with more individualistic patterns, such as single-family dwellings and homesteading. Some of the most dedicated and level-headed "back to the landers" have managed, through sheer hard work and much good fortune, to make a success of life in the countryside, and have also made a real impact upon the culture, agriculture and ecology of their chosen regions.

The accomplishments of this back-to-the-land movement have been extremely haphazard, though; at best, its experiments only represent small and isolated pockets of resistance in a jungle of ignorance and corporate bulldozers. If city people want to move to the country and enjoy rural life, they can often attain the individual inner joy alluded to by poets, but the belief that by doing so they are laying the seeds of the "New Society" is an illusion. Rural communal experiments have had little influence on the inhabitants of cities, where the majority of people now (or shortly will) live. The point is that the "free society" cannot be created in isolation from the mainstream urban culture—rather, it must be created *within* it, rising like a green Phoenix out of the ash-phalt of the megalopolis.

The Principle of
Bioregional Federation

In advocating regional organization and the self-governing community, we are not claiming that the transition from the nation state will be simple. One of the major problems is that existing social, environmental, and economic difficulties frequently originate outside the community; so, they cannot be solved at purely local levels. Thus the need for federation, the subject of this essay.

An example may clarify the matter. The chemical soup known as the Danube originates in Switzerland and passes through more than half a dozen countries. The problem of cleaning up its pollution has, unfortunately, been dumped on the downstream countries, despite the fact that they did not create the mess. This problem is compounded by the fact that the towns and cities along the river's banks are controlled by seven different centralized state bureaucracies. Given the importance of this major watershed to the ecology of Europe, the sanest way to address the Danube's problems would be to form a federation of all the communities along its banks. Although cohesion among such a diverse group would be difficult to achieve, it makes much more biological sense to unify around this common geographical feature than to continue the fruitless nationalistic bickering now taking place.

In a metaphorical analysis of the global water (hydrological) cycle titled *The Story of the Brook*, anarchist geographer Elisee Reclus suggests the direction in which humanity and nature must evolve with one another:

> Peoples mix with other peoples like brooks with other brooks, rivers with rivers; sooner or later they will form a single nation, just

as all the waters of the same basin finish by merging into a single river. . . . Humanity, until now divided into distinct currents, will be no more than a single river and, reunited into a single flow, we will descend together toward the great sea where all life will lose itself and be renovated.[1]

Social anarchists clearly do not call for complete self-sufficiency or community isolation; rather, they recommend that society be organized from the bottom up, based upon the natural bio-geography of the Earth. Any resulting federations would be voluntary associations of local groups formed to address common needs and problems. This principle lies at the heart of anarchist organization: in place of *centralization,* anarchism calls for the *federalization* of all dimensions of human activity–cultural, social, economic, political, recreational, and environmental.

This principle of federation is based upon observable processes in nature and society. It was first introduced as a political and economic concept by the early 19th-century anarchist P.J. Proudhon, then integrated into anarcho-evolutionary theory later in that century by Peter Kropotkin in his book, *Mutual Aid.* Although he did not deny the role of competition, Kropotkin stressed the importance of cooperation and interdependence in the evolution of biological life. Recent theory in ecology and evolutionary biology has confirmed the essential truth of Kropotkin's assertion that cooperation is more important than competition in the evolution of living organisms. For example, we cannot easily digest our food without the presence of certain bacteria in our guts, which in turn derive benefits from their presence there (a relationship known as *symbiosis*). Conscious or not, cooperation is a tactic that has been successfully adopted by a large proportion of animals and plants—dolphins, humans, elephants, and wolves are all examples of social species for whom the necessity of cooperation has led to increased intelligence.

The massive development of science in the late 20th century has led to new and exciting hypotheses about the development of life on Earth. The theory of mutual aid first proposed by Kropotkin is most dramatically illustrated in new discoveries in microbiology. The extraordinary patterns of information exchange and symbiotic development among microscopic bacterial life are truly astonishing, and certainly deserve attention from the general public and anarchists alike. In their book, *Microcosmos: Four Billion Years of Evolution from our Microbian Ancestors*, Lynn Margulis and Dorian Sagan argue convincingly for the centrality of cooperative processes in the evolution of life on Earth.

Even though life has existed on Earth for over three billion years, for the first half of that time the only life forms were simple, unnucleated cells which survive today as bacteria. Thus, for over a billion years after the advent of life, the Earth was covered with nothing but steaming pools of brightly colored microbes. The study of fossilized rocks and bacterial reproduction has revealed that not only has bacterial life been around for much longer than previously thought, but also that symbiosis and federation figured centrally in the evolution of life.

Bacterial cells are very simple organisms, with perhaps 300 times fewer genes than the nucleated cells of which we are composed. They compensate for this deficiency by freely exchanging tiny scraps of DNA among themselves and by digesting other bits of DNA from nearby damaged or dying cells. With their ability to create genetic variation by swapping tiny bits of matter "horizontally," bacteria can respond to environmental changes with great rapidity. Such efficient patterns of intraspecies symbiosis are evident in bacteria's now all-too-common resistance to penicillin and other antibiotics. (On the other hand, without bacteria to recycle our organic waste, the biosphere would cease to exist.)

They developed these capabilities, Margulis and Sagan suggest, as a defense against both high levels of solar ultraviolet radiation and volatility in the Earth's crust three to four billion years ago (due to volcanic eruptions and meteor impacts). In order to deal with continual damage from a life-hostile environment, bacteria were forced to adapt—to learn the trick of repairing themselves from bits and pieces of the decaying cells around them. The collective response of unicellular bacterial life over billions of years of evolution has thus been to develop the potential for a flexible, near-instantaneous (in evolutionary terms) exchange of genetic information–ultimately leading to bacteria's ability to regulate the chemical and organic composition of the biosphere for their own benefit.

Although Margulis and Sagan do not use the term "social anarchism" in their analysis, Bakunin, Kropotkin or Malatesta would almost certainly have concurred with their conclusions about the "decentralized," "self-regulating," "social" and "democratic" nature of bacterial life:

> As we move from a purely medical view of microbes to an understanding of them as our ancestors, as planetary elders, our emotions also change, from fear and loathing to respect and awe. Bacteria invented fermentation, the wheel in the form of the proton rotary motor, sulfur breathing, photosynthesis, and nitrogen fixation, long before our evolution. They are not only highly social beings, but behave as a sort of worldwide decentralized democracy. Cells basically remain separate, but can connect and trade genes with organisms of even exceedingly different backgrounds. Realizing that human individuals also remain basically separate but can connect and trade knowledge with very different others may be taking a step toward the ancient wisdom of the microcosm.[2]

Margulis and Sagan suggest that worldwide computer-assisted information exchange networks and other mutual aid associations are the most recent manifestation of symbiotic evolution. They see these trends as evidence for a universal tendency toward reciprocity, mutual aid, and "strength-in-unity." Their book concludes with a passionate appeal for global environmental cooperation combined with a vaguely formulated vision of freely federating communities linked by complex networks of information exchange. This vision has much in common with that of many prominent 19th century anarchist thinkers, notably Elisee Reclus and Peter Kropotkin (see Kropotkin's *The Place of Anarchism in Socialistic Evolution*).

Anarchists argue that rather than ameliorating conflict in human society, government has undermined the natural potential for intercommunal and social cooperation by creating inappropriate and socially alienating centralized power structures. The world has been artificially divided into mutually hostile states, many with vast military arsenals, with the United Nations the only solution proferred by national governments to date. It is difficult to say whether this body's current ineffectiveness or its potential strength as a coercive world government represents the greater threat to human survival. Social anarchists do not believe that a handful of bumbling officials playing God can ever hope to understand, let alone efficiently administer, our enormously complex social-ecological world. As we have seen, organic life developed by means of a non-centralized and self-organizing process of local adaptation. Large-scale, centralized human power structures headed by power-hungry generals, corporate bosses, and political hacks run contrary to natural evolutionary trends.

Social anarchists recognize that non-governmental and voluntary organizations are already vitally important and pervasive components of human social life. Every day, thousands of associations form and dissolve—social clubs, food cooperatives, carpools, playgroups, support groups, scientific and professional bodies, literary and artistic circles, bicycle clubs, fitness groups, and many others. Indeed, in every period and in every culture members of our species have associated, cooperated and federated with one another on the basis of mutual interest and concern–without feeling the slightest need for governmental control or coordination. Today, a vast pool of non-governmental and non-capitalist groups thrive in all areas of human life. Some *ad hoc* organizations last only a few days in order to meet the needs of the moment, while others cross oceans and develop into permanent, international federations. Anarchists hope that the eventual disappearance of capitalism and the nation state will allow the full federative potential of our species to flower. For every human need—economic, social, spiritual and recreational—some organization spontaneously develops.

Indeed, the modern communications and technological revolutions make the anarchist vision of a global federation of self-governing bioregions even more practicable than when first proposed over a century ago. Such bioregions would be linked by complex communication networks connecting a multitude of freely evolving mutual aid associations designed to meet human needs that could not be met at the level of the community.

This process is already occurring in many places. The "Tanami Descent Aboriginal Artists Network," creating satellite linkages among widely dispersed artists across Northern Australia's vast deserts, has now been expanded to link widespread tribal units, and is even being transmitted to some of their members in jail. Similarly, the emerging "computer cottage" phenomenon in the United Kingdom, whereby companies parcel out work to individuals who live in the countryside, has recently gained much media attention. Radio School in Australia and the Open University in the U.K., although not viable, long-term substitutes for schools and universitites, have nevertheless successfully educated isolated or busy people for many years.

The triumph of community and bioregion so necessary to the survival of our planet will require new (and, paradoxically, ancient) forms of organization. Social anarchists believe that federalism is a natural (and easily observable) form of organization that will meet human needs much more efficiently than have the centralized state administrative pyramids of the past.

"Think globally, act locally" is unquestionably the slogan that encapsulates the direction that human consciousness and activity must take. The kind of feeling that one has for one's ecoregion is qualitatively different from that which one has for one's country. "Love" of the nation state is the result of displaced kin loyalties, historical conquest, centralized domination over the local region, and lifelong exposure to nationalistic propaganda. Bioregional consciousness, on the other hand, results from the deeply felt human need for a sense of place, a sense of home. While nationalism has been a major obstacle to the realization of global environmental consciousness, the need to care for the land is an ethic that admits of no borders. In the act of caring for one's bioregion, one is at the same time caring for the planet and for the good of all beings. That is, acting locally involves not only *thinking* but *acting* globally.

It is obvious that the only organic and harmonious way to solve our global problems is to dissolve both the nation state and the United Nations. This is not to say that many of the functions which the United Nations performs are not necessary, but that they could be, and in some case already are, duplicated by non-governmental organizations. Organizations like the Red Cross impartially provide health care whenever and wherever needed; OxFam likewise helps the poorest women and children throughout the world. Non-governmental environmental groups such as Greenpeace monitor and expose environmental abuses around the globe. World cultural, sporting, and scientific associations investigate and participate in an immense variety of matters. All of this exists as part of the social infrastructure. Social anarchists hope that with the rise of telecommunications the number and influence of global mutual-aid networks will increase a thousandfold. We foresee countless groups created for peace, arbitration, and for all manner of cultural and scientific pursuits which will effectively ensure global cooperation. At that point there will be no need for an artificial and potentially totalitarian world government, or for the United Nations.

The idea that human settlement should begin at the level of the little brook, then federate along river basins or watersheds, all of which eventually join in the ocean, the source of all life, represents the mode of traditional human settlement—witness the growth of human community along the Nile and Yellow rivers. It is an idea found in the works of all the great philosophers and in many of the great religions of the world. The fundamental contribution of the anarchist geographers was to insist that, if it was to achieve harmony with the Earth, human political organization must abandon centralized control and instead organize the flow of human life along natural geographic features.

---

1. quoted by Garry Dunbar in *Elisee Reclus*, p. 52.
2. Margulis and Sagan, p. 96.

Anarchism, Chaos Theory, and the Metaphysics of Nature

Historically, anarchists have all too often been written off as advocates of chaos and disorder. Although this is, and always has been, far from the case, anarchists have characteristically been fascinated by the complexity of spontaneous natural order. This preoccupation has been largely vindicated with the development of modern chaos theory. Of course, this vindication is mitigated by the fact that one cannot directly equate human social interactions with mathematical theories, but the findings of chaos theorists are very suggestive nonetheless.

People have always noticed the entrancing, strangely organized swirling patterns displayed by smoke passing through a ray of sunlight. It is, however, only recently that we have developed computers capable of mathematically simulating and mapping the patterning of such complex dynamic systems—where every swirl of smoke affects the next in a never-ending orgy of integration and disintegration. Until machines were capable of performing the staggering number of computations necessary to mathematically understand complex order, we were simply unaware of this fascinating area of modern mathematics. Complex self order officially didn't exist until quite recently, because it was scientifically beyond proof. Whether these computer-generated programs really match the complex reality of a living environment is, of course, questionable. But experiments simulating the evolution of complex order from a very large number of a few different types of simple units, initially using a small number of very basic programmed rules, have produced intriguing results.

In recent years, computer-assisted mathematicians have attempted to simulate the evolution of life. They do this by placing short strings of letters in various combinations, with varying catalytic and reaction strengths assigned to each letter, each of which is capable of spontaneously joining up with one another to form longer chains. These simple chains of letters are designed to mimic small molecular chains of living matter reacting with one another in the "primeval soup." Computer-generated "auto-catalytic set simulation for the origins of life" suggests that a critical level of complexity was achieved in the "soup" by the lengthening of long strings of interacting polymers, eventually closing the loops and forming themselves into self-organizing webs. It seems that when systems reach a certain critical level of self-organized complexity, they are capable of undergoing qualitative and irreversible change in the direction of ever-greater levels of complex and cooperative order:

Traditional biochemistry has generally dissected life down to the last molecule and broken life down into its basic components, rather than attempting to understand how they came together in the first place. Computer-generated environments are doing the latter; they artificially simulate the synthesis of life using electronically and mathematically generated molecule-symbols programmed with simple rules under conditions favorable to the development of complex self organization—without actually programming the complex result.

Scientists don't claim to be actually producing life, of course. The development of complex webs out of single random strings represents at best a kind of artificial proto-organism, incapable of reproducing. The computer programmer programs the different "boids" or "molecules" to act in a particular way and alters the environment to see how they react individually and collectively to varying conditions. Complex patterns of dynamic order are not comparable to an organism, as they do not need nutrition, and are neither capable of producing offspring nor of genetically encoding them with the same simple rules of behavior with which they have initially been programmed. Rather, what scientists claim to have shown is that "life is not a property of matter per se, but the dynamical self organization of that matter. Its operating principle is that the laws of life must be laws of dynamical form, independent of the details of a particular carbon-based chemistry that happened to arise here on Earth four billion years ago. . . . The idea of viewing life in terms of its abstract organization is perhaps the single most compelling vision of the science of complexity."[1]

Although the actual details of a dynamic pattern cannot be ascertained in advance, complex order can be predicted to emerge somewhere at the "transition point" between simple order and absolute chaos. This claim is supported, in my view, by the fact that dynamic organization can be scientifically measured through means other than computer-generated systems. Ilya Prigoigine (winner of the 1977 Nobel Prize in physics for his work on dynamic non-linear systems) suggested in his book, *Order Out of Chaos*, that if you placed millions of ping pong balls in an enormous tank and blew air through them, they could eventually begin to develop orderly and complex patternings if we were lucky enough to reach a certain level of criticality.

M. Mitchell Waldrop reports on a similar experiment undertaken by Danish-born physicist Per Bak, who observed the action of dropping sand onto sand piles. Bak concluded that any mass of "simples," if they achieve a certain level or fluidity and order, can "move spontaneously to self-organized criticality." The results of Bak's experiments have also been successfully simulated on a computer screen. Following from these conclusions, Waldrop claims that:

> The most surprising lesson we have learned from simulating complex physical systems on computers is that complex behavior need not have complex roots. Indeed, tremendously interesting and beguilingly complex behavior can emerge from collections of extremely simple components. . . . The way to achieve lifelike behavior is to simulate populations of simple units instead of one big complex unit. Use local control instead of global control. Let the behavior emerge from the bottom up, instead of being specified from the top down. And while you're at it, focus on ongoing behavior instead of the final result, as living systems never really settle down. By taking this bottom-up idea to its logical conclusion, you could see it as a new and thoroughly scientific version of vitalism—the ancient idea that life involves some kind of energy, force, or spirit, that transcends mere matter. The fact is

that life does transcend mere matter, not because living systems are animated by some vital essence operating outside the laws of physics and chemistry, but because a population of simple things following simple rules of interaction can behave in eternally surprising ways.[2]

As an anarchist and a rationalist, I feel tremendously excited by modern chaos theory in that it claims to have shown that complex self-order is not created by God, but rather creates itself, developing from the simple to the complex rather than from the complex (god) to the simple. But as an anarchist I cannot help but feel disgusted that these observations are credited to Adam Smith and to the quasi-religious notion of vitalism; omitted are Bakunin and Kropotkin, both of whom argued that life and society are self-organized and should be left to organize "from the bottom up," in harmony with the peculiarities of local social and environmental conditions.

Such is the state of modern science—chaos is all the rage. Anarchists have been accused of advocating chaos for two centuries, but despite all the hoopla about this extremely interesting area of mathematics and environmental science, scant attention has been paid by scholars to anarchism's contribution to chaos theory. The great 18th century utopian philosopher Charles Fourier certainly explored a great many of the social implications of environmental diversity and complexity in his writings. And it is through exploring Kropotkin's philosophical writings on natural order (which owe an immense debt to Fourier) that I wish to redress this shameful gap in the scholarship of the history of modern chaos theory.

Noncentralized Organization Versus Centralized Organization

Many people still believe that organization and stability must be the result of some central organ, some centrally concentrated source of organizational force. This power, they think, must be embodied either individually, in the tribal chief or patriarchal father, or centrally, in the state. They believe that nature and the universe are organized by God, the tribe by its chief, society by the state, and the body by the brain. Natural, societal, and bodily organization must, it is assumed, be concentrated, enforced, and imposed by some omnipotent being or centrality. Society, without some concentrated organizational force or nervous system "radiating from Paris or from Berlin as far as the most remote game keeper, and ruling the most distant hamlet by orders from the capital" will, it is thought, simply disintegrate (Kropotkin, *Revolutionary Studies*). In *Anarchism: Its Philosophy and Ideal*, Kropotkin discusses the role of astronomy in the evolution of this belief:

> There was a time when man imagined the earth placed in the center of the universe. Sun, moon, planets and stars seemed to roll round our globe; and this globe inhabited by man represented for him the center of creation.
>
> An immense change in all conceptions of the civilized part of mankind was produced in the sixteenth century, when it was demonstrated that, far from being the center of the universe, the earth was only a grain of sand in the solar system . . .
>
> Take any work on astronomy of the last [18th] century. You will no longer find in it our tiny planet placed in the center of the universe. But you will meet at every step the idea of a central luminary—the sun—which by its powerful attraction governs our planetary world. From this central body radiates a force guiding the course of the planets, and maintaining the harmony of the system. Issued from a central agglomeration, planets have, so to say, budded from it. They owe their birth to this agglomeration; they owe everything to the radiant star that represents it still: the rhythm of their movements, their orbits set at wisely regulated distances, the life that animates them and adorns their surfaces. And when any perturbation disturbs their course and makes them deviate from their orbits, the central body re-establishes order in the system; it assures and perpetuates its existence.
>
> This conception, however, is also disappearing as the other [Earth-centered] one did. After having fixed all their attention on the sun and the large planets, astronomers are beginning to study now the infinitely small ones that people the universe. And they discover that the interplanetary and interstellar spaces are peopled and crossed in all imaginable directions by little swarms of matter, invisibile, infinitely small when taken separately, but all-powerful in their numbers. . . .
>
> The whole aspect of the universe changes with this new

conception. The idea of force governing the world, preestablished law, preconceived harmony, disappears to make room for the harmony that Fourier had caught a glimpse of: the one which results from the disorderly and incoherent movements of numberless hosts of matter, each of which goes its own way and all of which hold each in equilibrium.

When we study the ecology of a natural system, be it a rainforest, a coral reef, or a grassland, we perceive neither internal nor external concentrations of organizational force; there is no king of the jungle, no lord over nature—there is only *interaction*. For example, the forest is a natural and complex web of alliance and antagonism, cooperation and conflict, symbiosis and dominance. In a forest, a particular fungus grows upon the rootlets of a particular tree, each giving and receiving in turn the nutrients they require. One animal specializes in eating the fruits of a specific species of plant, thereby helping spread thousands of seeds. Two species are in constant conflict for resources, from which conflict a third species benefits, etc.

Natural systems at whatever level—even the biosphere itself—must be represented as dynamic organizational configurations, as stabilities of enormous complexity, in which life "without being subordinated to a central organ" is held in a subtle balance of conflict and interrelationship. Organizational force is dissipated and widely dispersed within a vast web of separate yet interdependent interactions.

Indeed, the very stability of a natural system develops and maintains itself precisely because there is no overriding or concentrated monopoly of organizational power. Each individual or species adapts its behavior to the dictates of an entire environment—the needs, energies, and habits of countless others. "Each," Kropotkin argues, "reacts on all the others."[3] Everything is adapted, ordered, and organized for everything else.

Kropotkin does not commit himself here to a naive "holistic" outlook in which nature is regarded as a seamless and unbroken whole. He does not contend that stability is the result of a fixed web of cooperation and symbiotic interrelations. Nor does Kropotkin idealize nature, for in nature areas of sustained interconnectedness and symbiosis are typically counterposed by areas of "reaction," "conflict," and "opposition."

Stability is not represented as an unbroken unity, but rather as homeostasis—a continuous "adjustment" and a "fugitive equilibrium" in which a "multitude of . . . automomous tendencies . . . balance and oppose one another continually."[4] Stability is a volatile disequilibrium held in balance through an ongoing interaction of diverse, and often autonomous, energies.

Internal Over External Organization

For many centuries, Western political and social theorists regarded a strong and external organizational force to be a necessary precondition for natural order. Rather than crediting the internal processes of nature itself for this order, they believed that it was created by an external deity that was above and outside nature. The theory of evolution destroyed this notion forever. Biospheric homeostasis, far from being the product of some mysterious, unknown force or authority, is now known to be the evolutionary result of an infinitely complex and astoundingly long process of self-organization.

Kropotkin's concept of complex self-regulation lies at the heart of our modern conception of natural process and stability. When we wish to preserve a piece of unspoiled wilderness, we do not begin by externally imposing some unnecessary order on it; rather, we automatically accept that it is internally self-organizing, and we accordingly attempt to disturb it as little as possible.

This principle of local self-regulation, Kropotkin believed, characterized not only large-scale organizational processes (e.g. the subtle rhythms of the seasons, the equilibrium of a rainforest, or the biospheric maintenance of sufficient oxygen), but was also observable in the smallest particles of organized living matter. For example, the human blood cell, though only a small part of a much larger and infinitely more complex entity, nevertheless exhibits some recognizable degree of self-organization. Indeed, even the smallest components of individual cells are, by virtue of their surrounding membranes, capable of regulating the flow of cellular nutrients, water, and wastes.

Building on his understanding of natural process, Kropotkin concluded that, in human society, the state is an unnatural entity.

For, although statist historians continually promote the idea that the historical function of the state has been that of benevolent organizer of some dark and primitive pre-social chaos, in reality its development has been intimately dependent upon the suppression and ultimate elimination of local, independent social life. To successfully fulfill its role, the state must first establish itself as the primary means of organization. The imposition of external state control thus necessitates the suppression of the local region or community. Even today, minorities and independent communities do not willingly give up their autonomy to the state; rather, they are forced to do so.

External organization is nearly always alienated from the natural and social systems upon which it tries to impose control. It is incapable of integrating itself with such systems' unique, and often highly complex, internal dynamics. Such alienation leads to misunderstanding, indifference, and intolerance. Subtle divergences and intricate internal associations are understood as symptomatic of chaos, rather than as evidence of internal order. Thus complexity is confused with disorder, variety with chaos, and uniqueness with defiance.

This confusion is what motivates the process of external classification and the imposition of uniformity. What is internally at variance with the state's imposed order must be repressed, leveled, and, if possible, eventually eliminated by brutalizing, external enforcement–always tyrannical, if not literally destructive.

Organization: From the "Simple" to the "Complex"

Instead of organizing society in a hierarchical fashion "from the top downwards," Kropotkin advocates the internal and horizontal organization of society "from the bottom upwards." He relies on the "simple" self-organization of particular localities, suggesting that such local units organize themselves through "free federation" into appropriately "complex" levels of organization as needed. In accord with this natural principle of local and internal organization, anarchists aim at the total abolition of the state. In Kropotkin's words, the state should be replaced by "social organization from the simple to the complex by means of free federation of popular forces . . . according to mutual agreement and to the infinitely varied, ever-changing needs of each locality."[5]

Fluidity Over Rigidity

For Kropotkin, spontaneity and turbulence were the two hallmarks of a living and developing system. He saw the universe in a continual state of flux; nature could not be conceived or represented as a static and unchangeable order. The organization of life necessitated an ongoing and spontaneous adaptation to the ever-modified demands of continued evolutionary change. Likewise, if human society is to remain vital and healthy, it has to continually develop and adapt:

> . . . The idea of stability, which was hitherto attached to everything which man saw in nature, is broken down, destroyed and put to naught! Everything changes in nature, everything [is] incessantly modified: . . . planets, climates, varieties of plants and animals, the human species—Why should human institutions perpetuate themselves?
>
> . . . What we see around us is only a passing phenomenon which ought to modify itself, because immobility would be death. These are the conceptions to which modern science accustoms us.
>
> But this conception dates almost from yesterday. . . . So much was the idea of immobility, of stability in nature, rooted in the mind [of medieval "man"] as in this epoch today continual change, evolution, is one of the most popular terms.[6]
>
> . . . The life of society we understand, not as something completed and rigid, but as something never perfect, something ever striving for new forms in accordance with the needs of the time. This is what life is in nature.[7]

Kropotkin recognizes the inadequacies of fixed and unalterable social laws and looks forward to

> . . . a society to which pre-established forms, crystallized by law, are repugnant; which looks for harmony in an ever-changing and fugitive equilibrium between a multitude of varied forces and influences of every kind.[8]

Diversity Over Uniformity or Homogeneity

Although a great deal of scholarly and intellectual attention has been focused upon Kropotkin's mutual aid theory, he never intended the theory to provide a comprehensive account of bio-historical development. Mutual aid was but "one factor" among many, and in any case was merely intended to serve as an exaggerated and rhetorical rejoinder to the Social Darwinist assertion that fierce, individualistic conflict represented the primary mechanism of evolution and progress. The history of social and biological evolution, Kropotkin claimed—and here he was far ahead of his time—was not comparable to a marching column with a single, overriding direction. Rather, it was better characterized as a multi-faceted development resulting from the growth of diverse and often conflicting tendencies. The evolution of life was not the product of a small set of unalterable evolutionary laws or mechanisms, but rather an ongoing and probabilistic process necessarily involving degrees of uniqueness, spontaneity, and irreversability.

Kropotkin saw the natural disposition toward spontaneity and variation, like the tendency of life at all levels to engage in cooperative and symbiotic behavior, to be of particular relevance to anarchist philosophy. Variation provides the material for evolutionary change and adaptation, and leads to the development of new species, through the processes of recombination and mutation, and new ways of surviving in a constantly changing world. Without variation and change, nature becomes static, immobile, and lifeless. Kropotkin exclaims, "Variety, conflict even, is life; uniformity is death."[9]

The stress which Kropotkin places on variation and diversification in nature is entirely consistent with modern concepts of evolutionary biology. Although some still regard cultural and biological evolution as steady, unidirectional progressions of ascension and elimination, leading to the eventual dominance of a single, superior species or culture, most scientists now see evolution as, simply, change—usually toward greater adaptation, complexity, and diversity.

Kropotkin suggests in the 1898 preface to *Fields, Factories and Workshops* that the organization of life "from the bottom upwards," "according to the infinitely varied and ever-changing needs of each locality," would create a cultural/environmental mosaic that would be more integrated with regional ecological variation, allowing for a more balanced and environmentally sustainable relationship with the natural world.

This view stemmed from his sophisticated understanding of evolution and of the complex, self-regulating natural world—and it's a view in perfect accord with modern chaos theory.

----

1. *Complexity: The Emerging Science at the Edge of Order and Chaos,* by M. Mitchell Waldrop. New York: Simon & Schuster, 1992. pp. 241-242.

2. Ibid., pp. 279-280.

3. *Anarchism: Its Philosophy and Ideal,* p. 120.

4. Ibid., p. 119.

5. Ibid., p. 133.

6. *Revolutionary Studies.*

7. *Modern Science and Anarchism.*

8. *Anarchism: Its Philosophy and Ideal.*

9. Ibid., p. 143.

Anarcho-Syndicalism, Technology and Ecology

In an anarchist society, the absence of centralized state authority will permit a radically new integration of nature, labor, and culture. As the social and ecological revolution progresses, national boundaries will become cartographical curiosities, and divisions based upon differences in geography, climate, and species distribution will re-emerge. This essay addresses the question of what role unionism will play in these changes.

First, it seems obvious that telecommunications, transportation, and postal networks all require organization which extends far beyond the individual ecological region, and activities like road building between communities require cooperation beyond that of individual locales. Thus, a return to a community-based lifestyle need not and cannot imply a return to the isolation of the walled medieval city or peasant village.

Anarcho-syndicalists (that is, anarchist unionists) argue that the best way to address such needs is for the "workers of the world" to cease producing for capitalist elites and their political allies. Instead, they should organize to serve humanity by creating not only communication and transportation networks, but industrial, service, and agricultural networks as well, in order to ensure the continued production and distribution of goods and services.

Yet there are many people in anarchist and radical environmental circles who regard anarcho-syndicalism with distrust, as they mistakenly identify it with industrialism. They argue that global industrialism has been responsible for centralized organization and environmental destruction. They view industrialism as necessarily based upon mass production, and the factory as inevitably involving high energy use and dehumanizing working conditions. In short, critics believe that providing six billion people with toilet paper and building materials (let alone TVs, VCRs, and automobiles) necessarily involves large-scale, mass production techniques ill-suited to ecological health—regardless of whether capitalist leeches or "free" workers are running the show. Industrialism, it is argued, is an environmental evil in and of itself; it is only made slightly more destructive by the narrow, short-term interests of capital and state. Such critics argue that technology has likewise outgrown its capitalistic origins, and has taken on a sinister and destructive life of its own.

I am not unsympathetic to this argument. That children and adults alike spend hours on end surrounded by deafening noise and blinding lights in video arcades, in an utterly synthetic technological orgy, is ample evidence of our species' sick fetish for non-organic, superficial pleasures. The regimentation of the work day, and the consignment of leisure and play to half-hour television slots interrupted by nauseating commercials, is nothing short of the industrial robotification of human nature—an alarming process that has led many to argue that humanity should abandon the industrial and technological revolutions altogether. They further argue that we should return to small-scale, minimally industrial technologies that utilize simple devices such as the hand loom. Given the enormously destructive effects of today's industrial system, such a course may ultimately be the only path open to humanity. At this point, however, simply abandoning our cities and our technologies and hoping that our species will somehow return to a small-scale, preindustrial existence appears both unlikely and reckless.

Worker Control

In recent years, there has been a revolution in the distasteful discipline of "personnel" management. For example, "experts" are declaring a new day in industrial relations because bosses now eat in the same canteen as the workers in some industries. In the past, when the bosses seemed to be distant figures, the inequities of the class/wage system were obvious to all. But if the bosses exercise with the rank and file in the company gym, they are perceived as "really just some of us." In such circumstances, workers tend to forget the 10- or 20-to-one pay differential, company car, and handsome retirement scheme that comes with being the boss. One example of this new type of "personnel management" is found in Australia, where there has been much fuss recently about a "harmonious, happy" outfit which "allows" employees to set their own wages, holiday arrangements, and production quotas. No wonder the boss is happy with this arrangement; s/he no longer has to go to the trouble of working all this out for them. Letting the workers spend their time figuring out the fine details of their own wage slavery is touted as the pinnacle of modern management techniques. (Not only would the employees be much better off financially if they sacked the boss and shared all the profits among themselves, their work would become a richly human experience instead of a dehumanizing and unrewarding one.) Merely by providing a *semblance* of an egalitarian work enviroment, modern management has dramatically increased production and minimized sabotage. Imagine the efficiency and satisfaction that would result if this appearance of worker control were turned into a living reality.

Efficiency and Self-Sufficiency

Although the local, small-scale production of manufactured items should be encouraged in every ecological region, it would be absurd to expect that every village, town or region would produce its own can openers, razor blades, nails, and windmill blades. Even if it were possible for craftspeople in every community to produce these products and thousands like them, this would surely involve an enormous waste of time and energy. No one wants to suffer the noise and clamor of the factory and be a slave to the machine, but neither do most people want to make their own nails and rope by the methods traditionally employed by village blacksmiths and rope makers. The hellfire and brimstone of the factory floor on the one hand, and hours of tedious, mind-numbing weaving on the other, are not desirable alternatives to the wire cutter and the mechanical loom, respectively. There is simply no good reason to reject industrial workshops as a means for producing the wide variety of manu-factured items that are required in our daily lives.

Only certain regions have the ores necessary to the production of iron, steel, copper and aluminum, and even if the manufacture of the many items made from such ores were carried out in each local region, it would still require a transport network to get the ores there in the first place. In adopting the ecoregionally self-sufficient community as the basis for a future anarchist society, we must not blind ourselves to its real limitations. In the absence of intercommunal worker associations for the provision of transport, communication, and basic articles of consumption, the anarchist vision is reduced to an absurd and unworkable utopia. Although we may justly assert that many items such as bread, food, energy, building materials, *ad infinitum* should, and in many cases could, be produced by the inhabitants of each city-region, insisting upon a concept of total self-sufficiency, as anti-syndicalist anarchists are apt to do, is unrealistic and dogmatic.

No one wants to spend their whole life in the factory or workshop, but everyone needs nails, transportation, or rope at some time. It would only be fair that all people spend a few hours every week helping to provide these useful products in cooperation with their fellows. Machines *do* help us make these things more easily; people only become slaves to their machines because they are slaves to their bosses and to a wasteful, growth-oriented economy. If there were no useless bosses who collect the profits but do no work at the machines they own or oversee, and if production did not always have to be increased to fuel an ever-expanding, growth-oriented consumerism, then it is doubtful that any of us would have to work more than a few hours per week. Those who are by temperament "workaholics" could spend their time improving upon and experimenting with products or projects of their choice.

Primitivism and Technophilia

Looking back toward the Stone Age or forward toward some postindustrial techno-utopia is equally pointless. Primitivists long for a quick fix from a (largely imagined) glorious past, while technophiles long for the quick fix in an idealized future—when the way out of the present mess probably entails an imaginative mixture of Neolithic community and selected technologies. For example, the use of non-renewable oil and coal resources during the past two centuries is undoubtedly ill-suited to the ecology of our planet, but so would be the Neolithic firewood hearth, were it to be used by Earth's six billion people today. (In time, all non-renewable energy sources will of necessity be superseded by renewable ones such as wind and water.)

The Bio-Industrial Revolution

But returning to the present industrial/technological night-mare, it seems evident that new technological priorities tend to produce changes of emphasis in the realm of so-called pure science. Biology was, until quite recently, seen as a "soft" science compared to the "hard" and more "logical" sciences of inorganic chemistry and physics. This is now changing, and the study of molecular biology is at the forefront of contemporary intellectual and popular interest. Botany, biology, and biochemistry are emerging as the main sciences of a second industrial age. Every day, natural products are being discovered that can take the place of the outdated, chemical synthetic materials of bygone eras. A doctor in one country discovers that a particular species of coral makes an excellent material for replacing lost or broken bone. A botanist in another country discovers a nut which produces an oil that can be substituted for a wide variety of inorganic chemcials. In New South Wales, farmers are experimenting with sorghum, fermenting it to produce ethanol—an environmentally clean car and tractor fuel. The sorghum and water by-products of this process are then used as high protein animal feed. Environmentally toxic paints containing lead or oil are being replaced by relatively harmless and easily biodegradable water-based ones—which not only make the job of cleaning up much easier, but also point toward a future when environmentally inappropriate industrial products will be replaced by more benign ones. Perhaps we can envision a time when every item of industrial manufacture presently associated with environmental destruction—cars, fuels, oils, aircraft, plastics, computers, etc.—is constructed with materials that have been harmlessly extracted from nature, and which can in turn be harmlessly and quickly reabsorbed by nature.

Capitalism and a Clean Environment

Industrialism is, however, beginning to partially reform itself. (Of course, environmental reforms under capitalism will succeed only to the extent that they are compatible with the profit motive.) Even our capitalist bosses cannot escape skin cancer and oil slicks while they sun themselves at their exclusive beach resorts; and many people no longer wish to buy or use environmentally unsound products. The capitalists, ever watchful of the market, have become increasingly aware of this fact; those companies which have presented a superficial "Green image" while persisting in unsound practices have on the whole been "found out," and are beginning to regret their dishonesty. Green journalism has created a better informed and extremely angry public which will no longer be easily fooled by transparent corporate tactics. Capitalists now fully appreciate that a Green image with genuinely Green products behind it will translate into big dollars and huge profits in the future.

Capitalists are not the only segment of our population undergoing Green-inspired change. Everywhere in the world inventors, scientists, engineers, and botanochemists are becoming inspired by the vision of a greener world, and the number of new and potentially environmentally safe processes and products multiplies with every passing day.

The year 1993 heralded the mass production of starch-based plastic products, which are able to disintegrate within a couple of weeks if left outdoors. Starch-based golf tees, takeout food containers, and those irritating little ties on packaged loaves of bread will be the first products to reach the marketplace; the potential of starch-based plastics seems almost limitless. Experiments with both old and new agricultural products are also showing much promise. In the future, a little-known plant called Cranbe will almost certainly be used to produce a wide range of industrial oils and plastics that may serve as substitutes for many hazardous petrochemically based products. The world slump in cereal prices is leading many farmers and companies to consider growing long-discarded crops such and flax and hemp, the natural fibers of which could replace the chemical foams used in chairs and mattresses. Rape seed oil is now being used as a base for glaziers' putty and, like water-based paints, is destined to make home renovation a safer and more pleasant experience. In the more tropical areas of the U.S., elephant grass is being considered as an energy crop. In the South Pacific, palm oil may soon be used as a substitute for diesel (which in most places must be imported at great expense) if certain minor technicalities can be overcome. Underwater windmills in the fast currents of New Guinea's Torres Strait could provide commercially useful quantities of electricity. Large blocks of the more conventional types of windmill are being considered for Australia's wind swept Red Centre. These examples represent just a few of the many possibilities for replacing artificial or otherwise harmful raw materials used in industrial manufacturing with natural or environmentally benign ones.

Consumerism and Environmentalism

Industrialism is not inherently anti-ecological, and the strength of Green consumerism will almost certainly ensure that the resource base for many of the manufactured products that we consume must and will change for the better. But the individualistic mass consumer culture which has grown up around the industrial system is another matter. If people continue to insist upon having three cars and individually owning every conceivable appliance and convenience, then things are unlikely to get very much better.

No environmentalist wishes to see many millions of acres of land devoted to the monocultural production of maize or palm oil in order to provide bio-fuels for our cars. But neither syndicalism nor, indeed, industrialism, require capitalism's promotion of "growth" and individualistic over-consumption. For example, syndicalists are committed to providing extensive public transport networks and other basic utilities on a non-profit basis for the benefit of all; and the provision of utilities or public transport using manufactured industrial products in no way requires the destructive and profit-oriented consumer culture of the present day. It might take X number of acres of biomass to power an electric railway, but it could well take 100 times that much to fuel the number of privately owned automobiles which would transport a similar number of people as the train. It might take Y amount of natural fiber to provide seating for that train, but it might take 100 times that much to outfit all of those cars. While it might be possible to grow enough biomass or fiber on small lots in a large number of small, organically diverse farms to support the train, the attempt to produce 100 times that amount to support the cars almost inevitably implies the need for extensive monocultural production—with all the degradation of wilderness and soil that such farming methods entail.

Capitalists are committed to growth oriented consumerism; it does not matter much to them whether they are selling natural or artificial products so long as people keep buying and consuming more and more. As a consequence, more and more of the available land is being given over to producing more and more products for *individual* consumption. Syndicalists, on the other hand, understand the need for the *communal* consumption of industrial resources. They understand that a well-constructed trolley line might last 100 years and transport millions or even tens of millions of people in its lifetime. Once a railway or trolley line is built, there is no inherent requirement for growth. Chances are, one line from point A to point B will be all that will ever be needed; there probably will be no need to construct another, let alone 20 or 30 of them. The point is that syndicalists are not interested in growth or profit, and their concept of industrialism must not be confused with the profoundly de-structive consumer culture of contemporary capitalism.

Anarcho-Syndicalism and Environmentalism

Only time will tell whether human technology and society can co-evolve successfully with nature. Neither the "primitivists" nor the "technophiles" can read the future, but I am convinced that neither alone holds the answer. That we can simply dismantle the industrial and technological r/evolutions and return to small-scale tribal communities seems even more naive a proposal than some old-fashioned anarcho-syndicalists' view that workers self-management alone will bring about the "free society." The idea that a workers' paradise could simply be built upon the shoulders of global capitalism is simply preposterous. The large-scale, centralized, mass-production approach that developed with capitalism, idolized by many marxists, was, unfortunately, never seriously challenged by either the union movement or by anarcho-syndicalists. The wider anarchist movement, however, has always distrusted large-scale, wasteful industrial practices and deplored the regimentation involved in work and the factory system, and has placed its faith in the self-governing, environmentally integrated community. Anarcho-syndicalists should review the intellectual insights of the broad anarchist movement to a much greater extent than they have. Otherwise anarcho-syndicalism will become just another tired, 19th-century socialist philosophy with an overly optimistic assessment of the liberatory potential of mass industrial culture.

Nevertheless, it is only through organizing our fellow wage-earners, who have the least to gain from the continued functioning of global capitalism, that we can build any lasting challenge to the state and its power elite. The traditional methods of syndicalism, such as the general strike, could bring the global megamachine to a complete standstill overnight. No other group can achieve this because wage-earners, and especially the growing army of service workers, represent the majority (at least 60%) of the adult population. Once the people wrest the industrial and service infrastructure from the hands of the elite, we can do what we will with it. Maybe the majority of workers will choose to dismantle their factories and abandon their fast-food restaurant chains, committing industrial mass manufacture to the dustbin of history; or perhaps they will elect to develop new, more localized versions of their industries. Of course, unless anarchists persuade their fellow workers to organize themselves to resist and eventually eliminate the current state and corporate coercive apparatus, this whole discussion is so much pie in the sky. This is the most compelling reason why an environmentally sensitive and rejuvenated anarcho-syndicalist movement represents one of the most practical methods of halting the destructive advance of the state and the mega-corporation.

The worldwide nature of pollution provides more reason for international workers' organizations. Even though governments have achieved some successes in controlling polution, these successes have been sporadic and limited. For example, the Montreal protocol appears to have been successful in slowing the continued production of ozone-depleting chlorofluorocarbons, or CFCs. These chemicals are, however, mainly produced by only six companies, and we should not be too optimistic about the possibility for global cooperation between capitalists and national governments on environmental issues. (The failure to do anything about "greenhouse" gas emissions shows the near-total lack of environmental concern of those in power.) Although CFCs were first synthesized in 1894, they were not used industrially until 1927. Had they been used beginning in 1894, we may not have had an ozone layer left to protect. We are told that, after a period of thinning, the ozone layer will most likely begin to repair itself. But what other longterm or irreversible industrial damage is occurring without our being aware of it?

The industrial system as we know it may indeed be causing such damage, but what do anti-syndicalist anarchists propose to do about it? Even if humanity decided to give up industrialism altogether and return to a craft economy, global cooperation among the industrial workers of the world would be necessary to implement that decision—via a permanent, worldwide general strike. In the absence of a grassroots and anarchistically inspired workers' movement that could mount a sustained opposition to industrial capitalism, such a course does not even present itself as a possibility. Anti-syndicalist anarchists, if they are sincere in their desire to abolish the industrial system, should as a matter of logic talk with working people, persuade them to accept their point of view, and then help organize them to implement it. Neither capitalists nor unorganized, unaware workers will abandon their factories and consumerist habits. And as long as there are industrial capitalists—and no massive international opposition to them—industrialism as we know it will assuredly remain.

Means and Ends

It is true that we may ultimately discover that most technology, and even the industrial system itself, is inherently environmentally destructive. It is even possible that many of the new eco-technologies that seem to offer hope may turn out to have unforeseen side effects, and that humanity will be compelled to give up modern technology altogether. But if this happens, it must be an organic process. Its starting point, one would hope, would not be simply to smash up the machines, dynamite the roads, and abandon the cities, beginning again at "year zero"—as Pol Pot attempted to do in Cambodia. The only non-authoritarian way in which the "year zero" can come is for the people to decide unanimously to destroy their factories, stores, highways, and telephone systems themselves. If this happens, there would be nothing anyone could or should do to stop them. But starvation, dislocation, chaos, and violence would almost certainly be the immediate result of such reckless actions, leading to dictatorship, horrendous suffering, and political and social passivity in the long run. (And even if primitivists would, by some miracle, convince a majority of our fellow citizens to discard science and technology, would that give them the right to force the rest of us to submit to their will?)

The everyday needs of humanity are enmeshed in the continued functioning of the industrial machine. One cannot simply smash up the life-support system and hope for the best. Instead, it must be carefully dismantled while new methods and practices are developed. If we are to achieve an eco-anarchist society, workers must wrest power from their employers, after which the goal should be production of socially necessary and environmentally benign goods. Once people are no longer forced to produce useless consumer goods and services, it is likely that every person will work only a very few hours per week—leaving people with much more time to devote to their own interests and to their communities. By eliminating the parasitic classes and reducing industrial activity to the production of basic necessities, a huge amount of human energy would be released. The reconstruction of the eco-regionally integrated human community from the corpse of the state could thus commence in an incremental way, ensuring that basic human needs would be effectively met while retaining the positive aspects of the industrial infrastructure. Each of us would have to continue to work a few hours per week to keep the industrial machine minimally functioning while we made changes.

If, in the face of sustained efforts to reduce its adverse effects and to integrate it with the local eco-region, the industrial system still proved to be an environmental menace, then humanity would, one hopes, have had the time to explore new ways of life suited to meeting its basic needs without industry as we know it. Industrial syndicalism is one relatively bloodless way of doing away with the state/capitalist elite and of allowing construction of an anarchist society; it may or may not have a place in the creation of an ecologically sound way of life, but it is a sure method of returning economic and industrial power into the hands of the people. Anarchists—be they industrial-syndicalist, technophile, or neo-primitivist—thus have no program other than to bluntly declare that it is the people who must decide their own social and environmental destiny.

Of course, the question remains of whether industrial syndicalism is the only, or most satisfactory, anarchist method of reorganizing the distribution of goods and services within communities. What we can be sure of is that the individualistic mass consumerism of the current state/capitalist system is quite ill-suited to the health and sustainability of life on Earth.

The Organization of Daily Life

In order to have influence, anarchists, who have always believed that the individual and the collectivity are of equal value and can coexist harmoniously, must clarify the alternatives to both capitalist and authoritarian "communist" economics. For example, nonprofit, community-based forms of individual skills exchange, such as barter-based networks, represent cooperative efforts which strengthen the autonomy of both individuals and communities. Local skills exchange systems use their own bartered "currency" and distribute goods, services, and labor within the community;

community infrastructures can thus develop according to the ideals of their members, without dependence upon government, capital, or state.

The value that ordinary people place upon individual effort and exchange cannot be ignored by anarchists; there is simply no need to collectivize or industrialize those services that do not require elaborate structures. Further, the rise of the service sector (counseling, food services, daycare, etc.), together with the need to reduce the work week and to minimize consumption by producing only socially necessary goods, will mean that the social organization of work will be increasingly directed toward community-based and non-profit activities such as skills exchange networks.

But unless the trains run and municipal water and energy supplies are assured, the social situation will quickly dissolve into chaos. The intercommunal postal and transport networks needed to deliver basic goods and services obviously cannot be supplied by community-based skills exchange networks. Again, anarcho-syndicalists' traditional approach to providing such services via worker-controlled organizations points to a solution: workers in non-profit industries would simply exchange their labor and products for credits in local skills exchange networks. Small-scale, non-industrial approaches and their integration with local exchange networks are thus viable steps toward an anarchist society. The realization of a federation of free communities requires a multi-faceted attack upon the institutions of capital and state, involving elements of traditional syndicalism as well as more individually oriented yet essentially non-capitalist systems of production and consumption, systems that allow for adequate levels of consumer choice.

Village life is in decline everywhere and, even if it will eventually be necessary to return to a world composed of small villages, at present we face the problem of increasing millions of urban dwellers living on the outskirts of cities which long ago ceased to be discernible social entities. The social ills upon which modern life is based—mass alienation, consumerism, and self-centered individualism—may prove fatal to our species, and should be democratically eradicated through education. Syndicalism, local skills exchange networks, and traditional cooperative ventures are ways of helping people to educate themselves about community and regionally based ways of life. These possibilities are far superior to either the Stalinist "proletarianization" of the people through terror, or the state capitalist robotification of the urban and rural masses by an endless media circus that lobotomizes people into insatiable consumerism, cynicism, and social apathy.

Anarchism, Ecology, and Human Population

The idea that the dramatic increase in human population is the primary cause of environmental degradation has become increasingly popular in the media. Media pundits and some "environmentalists" tell us that the most dangerous threat to planetary survival is, simply, "too many people." Thus, the right-wing, mechanistic, pseudo-scientific beliefs of some 19th-century social theorists—most notably Malthus—are regaining currency, even in certain environmental circles.

Frequently, off-the-cuff remarks by environmentalists about population or immigration are seized upon by the press and quoted out of context as evidence of Green racism or fascism. But such remarks often *do* reveal truly reactionary attitudes. For example, many people in the (non-radical but Green-oriented) Australian conservation lobby wish to halt *all* immigration on the "environmental" grounds that the country is already over-populated. Such attitudes can only do great damage to the radical Green movement. Similarly, some argue that human populations, like some other animal populations, must follow "boom and bust" cycles as do locusts or caterpillars. Third World starvation, land degradation, and pollution, rather than being the result of capitalism and anti-ecological lifestyles, are, we are told, merely the result of natural population pressures.

This crude linking of elementary population biology with grossly reductionistic, politically biased sociological analysis must be challenged, since it is a dangerous ideology with fascist overtones. Humans are reflective social beings who have the power to self-regulate their numbers and their social systems; locusts do not have this ability. And no intelligent person today would deny that overpopulation problems among some non-white groups are the result of socioeconomic oppression, not genes. One need only look at the modest level of one to two million at which the Australian aboriginal population has remained for the past 40,000 years to realize that human populations are indeed capable of attaining and sustaining optimal, but not necessarily maximal, sizes.

Before the development of capitalism, natural abundance was the pervasive feature of most regions in the world. The American prairies were home to hundreds of millions of buffalo, and the grasslands of Africa hosted a multitude of large animals. The Murray River in Australia was awash with gigantic Murray cod, and American rivers were likewise filled with salmon. It remains true that, treated with care and respect, the Earth is capable of supporting enormous populations of large and small animals; likewise, the existence of 5, 10, or even 15 billion people—although an undesirably large human population—does not in itself imply the degradation of nature.

The problem lies not so much with the number of people but with the anti-ecological lifestyles fostered by the capitalist economic system. For example, human population pressure has undoubtedly had some effect upon the decline of African elephants, since they need a lot of space and conflict with agriculture. The virtual elimination of 10 million elephants by the end of the 1980s, however, resulted more from avaricious ivory trading than peaceful human settlement and expansion. Drift netting, cattle ranching, river pollution, and industrial logging are other practices that deplete species numbers.

In a sense, there is not so much a population problem as a consumption problem. The postwar years have seen an explosion of individual acquisitiveness—everyone must own two cars, a color TV, a VCR, a washing machine, and a virtually lifeless lawn—in stark disregard for the collective effect of such items upon society and nature. A sharing of domestic resources, a little thought, and community energy is all that would be required to overturn this dangerous cult of consumerism. Rather than each family or individual building a castle, families and individuals could, together, construct the self-sufficient city. Rather than laboring to achieve individual consumer success, we could work for the provision of basic public goods and services for all.

Food is *the* most basic necessity of life, and democratically controlled food production should once again become a focus of our daily lives. People from both town and country must learn to give up lawns and monocultural, pesticide-driven agribusinesses, replacing them with aesthetically pleasing organic gardens and farms. The hugely degraded and treeless soils of wheat belts and range lands await regeneration by the careful, diligent work of rural peoples; even our urban nature strips and parks could provide a feast for ourselves and other species. Through "edible landscaping" in every available nook and cranny of our topography, we could ensure the availability of healthy foods for all people—and increase the base upon which natural abundance may once again flourish.

The idea that hunger is caused by scarcity due to over-population is simply a lie. In their pioneering and meticulously researched study of world hunger entitled *Food First,* Frances Moore Lappe and Joseph Collins succinctly state the truth regarding the world availability of food:

> Measured globally, there is enough food for everyone now. The world is producing each day two pounds of grain—more than 3,000 calories and ample protein—for every man, woman and child on Earth. This 3,000-calorie estimate, more than that consumed by the Western European, does not include the many other nutritious foods people eat—beans, nuts, fruits, vegetables, root crops, and grass-fed meat. Thus, on a global scale, the idea that there is not enough food to go around simply does not hold up.[1]

Even this statistic does not fully explain the true state of affairs regarding the realtionship between land and world hunger. The stark fact is that the people who own and control most of the arable land choose *not* to cultivate it:

> In most countries where people are hungry, large landholders control most of the land. A study of 83 countries showed that 3% of all landholders control a staggering 79% of all farmland. . . . Many who hold large amounts of land do so for prestige or as an investment, not as a source of food, and leave a considerable acreage unplanted. Moreover, the wealth produced is invariably not reinvested for rural development but drained off for

conspicuous consumption and for investment in industries catering
to the fancies of urban and foreign well-to-do. . . . In both Africa
and South America less than 20% of the potential arable land is
cultivated.[2]

Instead of being cultivated, much of this land is left as
permanent pasture for livestock. Those areas which are cultivated
(usually the most fertile and easily irrigated) are invariably not
used to grow staples for local use, such as rice or millet, but
rather are used to grow cash crops such as tobacco or cocoa, or
to produce low nutrition and luxury crops—asparagus, cucumbers,
strawberries, tomatoes, pineapples, or flowers—for affluent homes
and overseas markets. Where "staples" are produced, these are
most often grown not to feed local people but to feed cattle in
order to provide beef for the rich. Cassava, for example, which
used to be considered a basic bulk food for the poor, is now
being exported by the shipload to feed European cattle.

Gross inequalities in land ownership and distribution resulting
from colonialism have not only signalled the end of ancient
horticultural systems and traditional village cooperation, but have
also created a situation in which the laborers who work the land
have no incentive to improve it. For example, before the British
arrived in what is now called Bangladesh, cooperative
embankment, and pond and irrigation channel construction,
ensured the retention of monsoon waters. This permitted the
planting of an extra crop each year, and provided a plentiful
supply of fresh fish for the people:

At present, most of the fishing waters are controlled by absentee
owners who are satisfied to sell a small quantity of fish at high
prices to a few well-off consumers. . . . But what incentives are
there for sharecroppers and laborers, who work 90% of the land,
to build and maintain draining and irrigation canals and
embankments when such investments would primarily benefit the
landowners. . . . Not surprisingly, only about 5% of the country's
cultivated land is irrigated. Simple irrigation, making the "dry
season" no longer dry, would amount to a doubling of the food
base. . . . Cooperation in digging and maintaining ponds was
common before 1793 when the British instituted the individual
ownership of land. Today in villages throughout Bangladesh we

sadly note many silted-up ponds, and canals hardly capable of holding much water. And they are no longer village ponds but private ponds. Village-wide cooperative work is impossible when less than 10% of the rural households own 51% of the cultivated land, and when almost half the families are deprived of land. . . In Bangladesh, as in many countries we are made to perceive as hopelessly poor, it is the extreme inequality of the control over productive resources that makes cooperative work difficult and thwarts production.[3]

The unequal distribution of land not only leads to the underutilization of arable land, but places extra strain upon fragile ecosystems by forcing landless people to attempt to farm unsuitable areas. Televised images of starving peasants standing beside eroded hillsides or overgrazed marginal lands do not represent local ignorance, but rather the misappropriation of prime agricultural lands by moneyed elites and transnational corporations. This has certainly been the case in the Amazon, where the government has sponsored rainforest destruction by peasant "pioneers" in order to avoid having to forcibly redistribute Brazil's bountiful agricultural land. In other parts of the world, the colonial carving-up of nomadic lands, taxes upon cattle (which led to the destruction of the barter economy and forced herders to produce more for sale), and the post-colonial fetishization of beef products by the rich (instead of the production of mixed herds of different and smaller animals, utilizing a variety of forage) have all led to the enforced abandonment of traditional and environmentally sensitive methods of animal husbandry.

The overriding cause of hunger, starvation, and environmental degradation, then—indeed, lurking behind the obvious lifestyle and technology factors—is the corporate capitalist system under which we are forced to live. Forty thousand children die each day from malnutrition, while peasants and tribal peoples are forced off their traditional lands by corporations anxious to grow profitable export crops such as tobacco, sugar cane, and coffee. The advance of corporate capitalism is unrelenting. For example, the "free trade" agreement between Mexico, Canada, and the United States provides a framework for the destruction of the *ejidos* (peasant cooperative village holdings) by corporate interests, and threatens to completely reverse the gains made by rural peoples in the Mexican Revolution.

Of course, not only do corporate capitalist industrial and agricultural methods degrade the land, they also fuel population growth. There is a proven correlation between extreme poverty and dramatic increases in population. When the English Commons began to be fenced in the 17th century, household poverty levels began to shoot up, followed by an increase in population. As Britain began to exploit the resources of its new colonies, however, revolution was postponed by a compensating rise in the living standards of its citizenry. The continued theft and destruction of land by European, American and, later, Japanese state and corporate bureaucracies led to extreme poverty in many parts of Africa, Latin America, India, and Southeast Asia. Although the population has now stabilized in most parts of Europe and the U.S., the lack of sufficient income, food, and health care in many of their former colonies is the single largest contributing factor to the startling increases in world population. When access to health services and adequate nutrition is low, infant and child mortality is high, and women tend to have as many children as possible so that at least some of them will survive. It has been demonstrated conclusively that most mothers, if convinced that health services, food, and security will be provided such that every child will have a very good chance of reaching maturity, prefer to restrict themselves to few, even one or two, children. By overthrowing corporate capitalism and returning land to the people, the population problem will be all but eliminated in those countries where hunger, misery, and death now reign supreme.

Although the attempt to link human sexual politics with environmental issues is sometimes misguided, it is obvious that sexual politics are necessarily an important component of the population problem. Recent evidence shows that, in addition to a continuing decrease in desired optimal family size since the industrial revolution (undoubtedly tied to decreasing infant morality rates and an upswing in living standards), a desire for female emancipation that actually preceded industrialization was an equally critical factor in the decline of European birth rates in the 18th and 19th centuries:

If industrialization and declining mortality were not completely responsible for declining fertility, then what else was? Increasingly the evidence points to another, initially independent revolution—the emancipation of women. The origins of this profound and continuing social movement probably can be found in the eighteenth century Enlightenment. Many of the leading voices of the Enlightenment were French, and although women were not central to their concerns, these thinkers legitimized the questioning of social and political roles, including those associated with patriarchy. The Enlightenment also fostered a sense of hope that through knowledge, the old world of predestination and fatalism would be replaced by one of freedom to shape human destiny for the better.[4]

Today, the "medicalization" of birth control—which denies basic human rights to women—is greatly contributing to frightening increases in human population. Birth control has been practiced in some form in virtually all societies, and is primarily an individual and social, not a medical, practice—that is, doctors and bureaucracies need not be involved. The use of condoms, diaphragms, and other forms of birth control involve the technical issues of how to produce and distribute them, the social issue of how best to get people to use them, and the individual issue of personal choice. These are not medical issues.

To maximize its effectiveness, contraception should be available in every marketplace, store, and supermarket, in every village, town, and city of the world, so that anyone, at any age, has unrestricted access to the contraceptive of her/his choice. Another key to lowering the birth rate is that such unrestricted access to contraceptives must coincide with a decline in patriarchal attitudes and an increase in willingness on the part of men to voluntarily utilize birth control (and to support its use by their partners).

The medicalization of reproduction has led not only to restricted access to contraception, but also to a kind of "soft (and sometimes 'hard') policing" of reproductive technologies by medical bureaucrats and state social workers. This has never actually controlled population growth over the long term, and has frequently led to sickening acts of cruelty. Authoritarian state sterilization programs such as China's one-child-per-family policy have met with limited localized success (especially in the country-side), but at the expense of individual health and choice (see PBS show, "China's Only Child"). In the Philippines, the government offers poverty-stricken women, starving for want of a decent meal, comparatively large amounts of cash to undergo sterilization. These operations are frequently performed in rural areas under extremely unsanitary conditions, with little or no aftercare, and have led to the deaths of large numbers of women who have undergone this humiliating experience. Finally, it has been shown that in many places in the Third World the husband's refusal to forego sexual intercourse or allow the use of birth control (often because of religious proscriptions) is the biggest obstacle to limiting pregnancies—an obstacle cited by women themselves.

Attempts to look at the population problem from a purely biological or "scientific" perspective, without careful analysis of class, race and gender structures, are at best naive and at worst positively dangerous. To blame an abstract biological notion of natural increase for overpopulating the world—when it is quite obviously caused by statism, patriarchy, and capitalism—suggests that a starving Somali refugee is as much to blame for overpopulation as a fat businessman or grossly overpaid World Bank official. Humanity must choose to develop the alternative lifestyles, social systems, and sexual practices that will lead to stable and sustainable population levels. But under the present system, such change is impossible to achieve without top-down, authoritarian methods, and use of such methods is no guarantee of success. Only freedom from hunger and ill health, plus the freedom of educated reproductive choice, can achieve the ecological integration of humanity with the rest of nature. Only a revolution in the economic, social, and agrarian realms, in concert with women's liberation from exploitative patriarchal and capitalist practices, can solve the present human population crisis.

----

1. p. 21.

2. *Food First*, pp. 21-22

3. *Food First*, pp. 26-28

4. "Fertility in Transition," by James L. Newman, *Focus*, Spring 1986, pp. 4-5

Anarchism & Social Ecology:
A Critique of Murray Bookchin

Murray Bookchin has deservedly emerged as a major thinker and writer in the late 20th century; and he is widely respected as one of the most important anarchist theoreticians of our time. His ideas about the relationship between social ecology, anarchism, and trade unions thus merit our close attention.

Although Bookchin has become openly hostile toward unionism and anarcho-syndicalism—and in fact to any class-based analysis—this has not always been the case. Some of his earlier writings on these subjects, though deeply critical of syndicalism, contained insightful comments upon the value of traditional anarcho-revolutionary theory and practice. The best example of his earlier thinking is found in his essay, "Self-Management and the New Technology," published in 1980. Here Bookchin argues that the syndicalist conception of the central role of factory or workplace in a future anarchist society reflects an overestimation of the liberatory potential of large-scale industrial activity. He rightly claims that the factory system has destroyed the craftsman and the artisan, and has degraded the dignity of work, through its reliance on mass production:

> Of the technical changes that separate our own era from the past ones, no single device was more important than that of the least mechanical of all–the factory. Neither Watt's steam engine nor Bessemer's furnace was more significant than the simple process of rationalizing labor into an industrial engine for the production of commodities. Machinery, in the conventional sense of the term, heightened this process vastly–but the systemic rationalization of labor to serve in ever-more-specialized tasks demolished the technical structure of self-managed societies and ultimately of workmanship–the "selfhood" of the economic realm.

. . . True craftsmanship is loving work, not onerous toil. It arouses the senses, not dulls them. It adds dignity to humanity, not demeans it. It gives free range to the spirit, not aborts it. Within the technical sphere it is the expression of selfhood par excellence—of individuation, consciousness, and freedom. These words dance throughout every account of well-crafted objects and artistic works.

The factory worker lives merely on the memory of such traits. The din of the factory drowns out every thought, not to speak of any song; the division of labor denies the worker any relationship to the community; the rationalization of labor dulls his or her senses and exhausts his or her body. There is no room whatever for any of the artisan's modes of expression—from artistry to spirituality—other than an interaction with objects that reduce the worker to a mere object. . . . Marxism and syndicalism alike, by virtue of their commitment to the factory as a revolutionary social arena, must recast self-management to mean the industrial management of the self. . . . Both ideologies share the notion that the factory is the "school" of revolution, and in the case of syndicalism, of social reconstruction, rather than its undoing. [Both] share a common commitment to the factory's structural role as a source of social mobilization. . . . The factory not only serves to mobilize and train the proletariat but to dehumanize it. Freedom is to be found not within the factory but outside it.[1]

Bookchin concludes that the factory system, the foundation of industrial syndicalism, is intrinsically authoritarian and dehumanizing. The syndicalists, he feels, have confused the factory, the "realm of economic necessity," with the "realm of social freedom," or community, and the liberated city. Contrary to the syndicalist vision, the factory should never be regarded as the locus of political action and freedom. In Bookchin's view, only the re-emergence of a nonhierarchical and economically just social existence will guarantee liberty and prosperity. He further argues that the coal-steel-oil technology upon which the factory system is based is no longer viable due to resource depletion.

Bookchin contends that solar, wind, and other renewable energy sources are most efficiently utilized on a local basis. An economic infrastructure consisting of a large number of small workshops, producing individually crafted tools from local, non-polluting power sources, would replace the industrial manufacturing system of the past. The factory is obsolete; it no longer belongs even to the realm of necessity—environmental determinants having rendered the factory system of industrial production ecologically, and thus economically, redundant.

Bookchin makes some valid points in this penetrating essay. For example, the pictures of thousands of workers—heads held high and anarchist banners in hand, marching out of row upon row of factories—that have until recently adorned our anarcho-syndicalist journals, exhibit a singular inability to appreciate the scope of both the ecological crisis and the emerging, global ecological consciousness. The reasons for this important oversight are historical and practical, not theoretical. At the end of the 19th century, a century that witnessed rapid industrial development, marxists and socialists regarded the eco-anarchist ideal of ecoregional self-sufficiency and town/country balance as too utopian or, alternately, as indicative of a backward-looking, pre-industrial ideology. In turn, anarchists saw fit to downplay the environmental aspects of their vision, and anarcho-syndicalists continued to focus upon establishing industrial democracy inside the factory, to some extent ignoring the wider ecological components of the anarchist tradition. Unlike marxists, however, anarchists have always shown interest in the proper relationship between industry and ecology—an early and famous example being Kropotkin's *Fields, Factories and Workshops.* Given our current ecological crisis, Bookchin is quite correct in stressing the importance of restoring anarchist theory's focus upon appropriate technologies and ecologically integrated communities.

Bookchin's essay was, however, written over a decade ago and, with the other essays in *Towards an Ecological Society,* it bridges the two phases of his writing and thinking: Bookchin the Anarchist-Ecologist of the 1960s and '70s, and Bookchin the Social Ecologist of the 1980s and '90s. (Notably, Bookchin the Social Ecologist is far less kind to anarchism and unionism than he could be.) His two pamphlets, *Ecology and Revolutionary Thought* and *Towards a Liberatory Technology* (both written in 1965 and reprinted in an anthology of his writings entitled *Post-Scarcity Anarchism*), are succinct and easily understandable statements of the ecological-anarchist viewpoint. In these early pamphlets as well as in his two later books (*The Limits of the City,* 1974, and

Toward an Ecological Society, 1980), Bookchin updated and enlarged upon many social-ecological ideas found in the works of past utopian and anarchist thinkers—notably Charles Fourier, Peter Kropotkin, and Elisee Reclus. He clearly and convincingly showed that, with its non-centrist and non-hierarchical prescription for a stateless order, anarchism is the only social philosophy capable of ensuring the long-term survival of our species and our planet.

Since the end of the 1970s Bookchin has been expounding his ecological philosophy, "social ecology." Although none of the basic tenets of Bookchin's social ecology are incompatible with anarchism, in his more recent works he mentions anarchy only in passing. Nevertheless, many things that Bookchin has to say are relevant to anarchists. This is especially true of his extended discussions of the role of patriarchy in creating a hierarchical, exploitative and anti-ecological social system—an issue that was underplayed by Peter Kropotkin and Emma Goldman in their analyses of the evolution of human authoritarian structures.

Bookchin's explicit rejection of the need for working class organization and trade unionism, however, signifies a widening philosophical gap between social ecology and the dominant trends in modern anarchism. Indeed, Bookchin seems to reject *any* form of class analysis. In the most accessible of his recent works, *The Modern Crisis*, he mercilessly attacks anarcho-syndicalism, the IWW, and unionism. Because its proponents insist upon class analysis and believe in the revolutionary importance of the industrial proletariat (even though modern anarcho-syndicalists consider almost all productive persons—from housewives, to service workers, to factory workers—as part of the "proletariat") anarchism, like marxism, seems to Bookchin just another tired, old, irrelevant socialist philosophy:

> The politics we must pursue is grassroots, fertilized by the ecological, feminist, communitarian and anti-war movements that have patently displaced the traditional workers' movement of half a century ago. Here the so called revolutionary ideologies of our era—socialism and anarchism—fall upon hard times. Besides, their "constituency" is literally being "phased out." The factory in its traditional form is gradually becoming an archaism. Robots will soon replace the assembly line as the agents of mass industrial

production. Hence future generations of industrial proletarians may be a marginal stratum marking the end of American industrial society.

The new "classless class" we now deduce is united more by cultural ties than by economic ones: ethnics, women, countercultural people, environmentalists, the aged, unemployables or unemployed, the "ghetto" people, etc. It is this "counter-culture" in the broadest sense of the term, with its battery of alternative organizations, technologies, periodicals, food co-operatives, health and women's centers, that seems to offer common resistance to Caesarism and corporatism. The re-emergence of "the people" in contrast to the steady decline of "the proletariat" verifies the ascendancy of community over factory, of town and neighborhood over assembly line. The hand fits the glove perfectly—and clenched it makes the real fist of our time.[2]

Exactly what sense are we to make of such sweeping dismissals of several centuries of sustained resistance to the encroachments of capital and state by ordinary working people? Anarchists and anarcho-syndicalists have, to my knowledge, always emphasised the need to foster community, and have never made the absurd claim that society could be "organized from the factory floor." It is simply wrong for Bookchin to claim that anarcho-syndicalism (let alone anarchism as a whole) has emphasized the historical destiny of the industrial proletariat at the expense of community and free city life. Anarchists have always emphasized that the primary unit of anarchist society should be the free, ecologically integrated city or town—how else could one hope to organize social life in the absence of the nation state? And just why wouldn't unions and workers' cooperatives—be they comprised of bakers, grocers, bus drivers, postal workers or daycare workers—be the natural, logical bodies within which ordinary working people would coordinate the economic and industrial life of *their* city? Members and potential members of trade unions and industrial unions are not just "the proletariat"; they are, rather, real people—feminists, peace activists and ecologists included. They join together to organize their trade or service in a spirit of equality, peace and cooperation.

Observing today's decline in manufacturing and heavy industry in his own country, Bookchin fails to appreciate the well-known fact that capitalist manufacturers have moved offshore. Rather than give in to workers' demands for higher pay and better conditions, capitalists in America and Australia have chosen to move their industrial plants into "newly industrializing" countries in Latin America, Southeast Asia, and elsewhere. In some of these countries, the state/capitalist push to industrialize has led to the mass exploitation of labor at near starvation wages, and the appalling abuse of female and child labor. The American union movement, long ago usurped by conservative elements (with the active aid of the government), has done very little—both in the U.S. and abroad—to combat these trends, and most Americans rightly perceive it as ineffective and outdated. Meanwhile, workplace organizers in Indonesia and Latin America regularly "disappear" or receive long prison sentences. Millions of people, including children, slave in sweat shops in these "newly industrializing countries," and, in doing so, undermine the wages and conditions in the "industrialized world." Capitalists insist that labor costs are too high at home, and call for working people to accept lowered wages and degraded working conditions in order to retain jobs and to compete with offshore enterprises. Virtual slave labor overseas is thus being used to manipulate workers and undermine the effectiveness of unions at home, while fledgling union movements in developing countries are ruthlessly suppressed.

Near instantaneous satellite communication and accounting technologies have allowed the industrialists to move their operations into the more stable areas of the Third World; increased transport costs are handsomely compensated for by negligible labor costs. Because anti-syndicalist anarchists fail to look beyond their own shores, they lack an appreciation of this global capitalist strategy designed to destroy working class organization. The industrial working class is indeed declining at home, but the mass proletarianization of, for example, the rural villagers of Northern Thailand, who are moving south to work in the new factories, is increasing. Meanwhile, world population continues to increase, and nearly everyone wants a TV and a car, while everyone needs can openers, clothes, cooking utensils, and other necessities. Because it is the working class who produce such items, it follows that, even given the trend toward automation, worldwide the industrial working class is increasing, not decreasing. The virtual outlawing of unionism in Indonesia should provide anti-syndicalist anarchists with ample evidence of the fact that the capitalist state will go to almost any lengths to prevent worker organization.

Developments within the service sector are also foolishly overlooked by Bookchin and other critics of industrial unionism. Hamburger slingers and supermarket personnel may not be industrial workers in the traditional sense, but they are certainly exploited workers. As jobs in manufacturing and heavy industry move offshore, large numbers of adult women (and increasing numbers of displaced adult male workers) are joining 14-to-17-year-old youths in jobs in the light industrial, clerical, and service sectors. Unfortunately, the adults are too desperate, and the teenagers too naive, to be easily organized. As new or existing unions begin to seriously undertake the task of listening to and organizing these workers, encouraging trends are emerging in the service sector that certainly should not be overlooked by anarchists.

So, although, thankfully, millions of people are no longer forced to claw at rocks with crude picks in the bowels of the Earth in order to make a living, I fail to see why Bookchin is confident that the *worker* is obsolete. If work itself is obsolete, how are the majority of our population—people who are not managers or well-educated professionals—going to support their families? How is anyone going to travel or phone another city in Bookchin's ideal world of liberated, self-sufficient city-communes unless we can construct, install, and repair the roads, railways and telephone cables? People will always want to send letters and packages to each other, and thus a postal service will always be necessary (and, if we ever colonize other planets, even more necessary!). Economic and industrial life are unmistakably global in nature; the idea that one could organize an intercontinental railway network from one commune or city alone is as absurd as the proposition that one could organize social life from the factory floor.

Industrial and service sector work is hardly likely to disappear; indeed, 60% of the United States adult population does such work. Anarchists simply state, realistically, that, in the absence of capitalism and the nation state, most workers will organize (or continue to organize) to control the work that they choose to perform—for the good of themselves, their city, their ecological region, and humanity. Most anarcho-syndicalists do not have tunnel vision; anarcho-syndicalism is a humanistic cluster of ideas that embraces decentralized self-government in all aspects of human social life—the free city, the agricultural cooperative, the household, the hobby group, *and* the workplace.

Bookchin is more constructive when he points to "the Green network" as providing a new and significant springboard to revolutionary transformation. Over the past 30 years, individuals and groups of people connected by nothing other than a love of the Earth have begun putting their philosophies into action. Local groups of horticulturalists growing native trees for free distribution, organic food cooperatives, forest action groups, and a plethora of specialized ecological journals, have been bringing together people of all races, classes, and ages. The local, popular, and decentralized nature of this Green networking represents a powerful and non-centralized force for social and ecological change. At the more radical end of the Green network one finds people who care deeply about the environment, but who have become disillusioned about the ability of the state/capitalist order to solve the urgent ecological problems of the day. This group has set out to save the planet by any reasonable means—legal or otherwise. They have flung themselves in front of bulldozers, whaling ships, and logging trucks. Their antics and exploits have captured the popular imagination, and they have had some success in saving portions of the wilderness from destruction.

But due to the lack of a significant working class power base, the efforts of radical environmentalists have resulted in few lasting victories. They are not getting their message across to their potentially most powerful allies—unionists and unorganized working people. Indeed, many of these people feel alienated from environmentalists' direct-action tactics, which appear to them to mock productivity and the American Dream, which they are often still striving to attain for themselves.

Inspired by a vision of a more just and equitable society, working class organizations have opposed capitalism and the state for centuries. The fact that these two forces are not only unjust and authoritarian, but also extremely environmentally destructive, only confirms the inherent wisdom of centuries of radical working class organization. The heroic resistance of working class organizations to state-sponsored capitalist exploitation represents a long and bloody history involving the useless murder and ruthless torture of millions of ordinary people, whose only crime was to attempt to protect their families, communities, and natural resources from being sacrificed for the short-term benefit of the rich and powerful. Radical environmentalists, in contrast, are relative newcomers to the art of organized resistance, and have yet to digest the hard historical fact that the institutions of state-sponsored exploitation cannot be defeated without the commitment of large sections of the majority of our population— that is, the poor and working classes—to the Green cause.

The tragic lack of communication between eco-activist groups and unions has deprived the ecology movement of an effective power base. It has led, for example, to the absurd situation in Australia of Green activists fighting with rank-and-file members of woodworkers' unions, whose members are unaware that gross corporate mismanagement, not latter-day conservation efforts, is the true cause of forest depletion and job loss. There is a lesson for both Greens and workers alike in these absurd showdowns— that the real enemies are the greedy and short-sighted institutions of capital and state, not our near-individually powerless fellow citizens. Both parties would be better served by joining together and working towards a grassroots, revitalized and ecologically informed union movement which, if not capable (for the time being) of overthrowing the forces of the rich and powerful, would at least be able to resist the worst excesses of the present order. That the welfare of working people is intimately dependent upon a healthy environment is an undeniable fact, and both eco-activists and unionists should try to improve their communication and to find common ground.

In advocating craftsmanship on the one hand, and large industrial plants run by robots on the other (in *Towards a Liberatory Technology*), Bookchin seems to contradict himself. He has never to my knowledge endorsed any kind of anti-technological viewpoint, which makes his anti-union stance all the more puzzling. How is one to design, manufacture, and recycle the environmentally friendly eco-technologies to which he so frequently refers without utilizing the skills and resources of industrial workers? Although working people now form the backbone of our profoundly destructive oil-steel-coal industrial culture, their proven skills could also turn munitions factories into wind generator manufacturing plants, and our agri-business wastelands into productive farms. The wise ecologist recognizes the need to move away from large-scale industrial activity, but knows that our present factories are the places, in cooperation with research institutions, that should begin to design and manufacture the eco-friendly technologies of tomorrow. A successful end to this period of transition and technological readjustment clearly cannot be achieved without the cooperation of the industrial workforce.

Bookchin goes on to insult American anarchists and trade unionists of the past. "These immigrant socialists and anarchists (presumably referring to such people as Emma Goldman, Alexander Berkman, and the Haymarket martyrs) "were largely unionists rather than revolutionary utopians," and had little understanding of America's democratic traditions. If the American people had ignored the "narrow" and "class-based" ideologies of these anarchist and socialist foreigners, and instead upheld the individualistic values of the American Constitution, concretely enshrined in the small town meetings of New England, an authentic American radicalism could, in Bookchin's view, have taken firmer root, and a decentralized vision of a free American republic could have become a reality:

> Irish direct action, German Marxism, Italian anarchism and Jewish socialism have always been confined to the ghettoes of American social life. Combatants of a pre-capitalist world, these militant European immigrants stood at odds with an ever-changing Anglo-Saxon society . . . whose constitution had been wrought from the struggle for Englishmen's rights, not against feudal satraps. Admittedly these "rights" were meant for white men rather than people of color. But rights they were in any case—universal, "inalienable rights" that could have expressed higher ethical and political aspirations than the myths of a "workers party" or the day dream of "One Big Union," to cite the illusions of socialists and syndicalists alike. Had the Congregationalist town-meeting con-

ception of democracy been fostered . . . and the middle classes been joined to the working classes in a genuine people's movement instead of being fractured into sharply delineated class movements, it would be difficult to predict the innovative direction American social life might have followed. Yet never did American radicals, foreign born or native, ask why socialist ideas never took root outside the confines of the ghettoes, in this, the most industrialized country in the world.[3]

Again, what sense is one to make of such comments? Bookchin accuses American radicals of the past of having a "ghetto" outlook, yet it is precisely this group of people—"ethnics," "unemployables," and "the 'ghetto' people"—whom Bookchin identifies in a passage quoted above as representing the new revolutionary "classless class" of people who will somehow organize the cooperative suburban communities of the future social ecological order. Ironically, it was the "ethnic," "unemployable" and "ghetto people" of the 19th and early 20th centuries, of whom Bookchin speaks so disparagingly, who led the movement to form unions, leading ordinary working people to fight for One Big Union.

Moreover, the specific organization to which Bookchin refers, the Industrial Workers of the World or IWW, was not, as he suggests, unappealing to "native" Americans. Rather, it was brutally and systematically smashed by the combined forces of federal and state military and judicial might. Many IWW organizers—and the members they signed up—risked life and limb and had little stake in the comfortable, middle-class vision of small town life of which Bookchin speaks.

Finally, in embracing unionism, anarcho-syndicalists do not, as Bookchin claims, have some naive or mystical faith in the ability of working class culture to save the world. They do not share the marxist vision of a workers' paradise; they merely say that if we want to create a more balanced and equitable world, a good place to start is in the workplace.

Groups of peace protesters and environmentalists singing songs outside nuclear bases cannot by themselves be an organizational basis for sustained national resistance to the state/capitalist system. Unless the telephones, railways, and other vital industrial systems continue to function from the moment the state/capitalist order begins to crumble, Bookchin's ideas will remain nothing but a pipe dream. Nor is the bringing together of millions of workers—in unions—in a general strike an end in itself; rather, it is the best vehicle for producing a movement that is capable of resisting military and economic monopoly, and, ultimately, of replacing the present order.

This is not to say that the industrial system which has led our planet to the brink of catastrophe need not undergo radical change, but rather that while it must undergo profound change, this does not mean that industrial unionism should disappear. On the contrary, an ecologically informed and regenerated union movement could do much to initiate the needed transformation. The boycotting of environmentally damaging substances and industrial practices, an insistence upon safe and healthy working conditions, the production of socially necessary goods and services based on need rather than profit, and a de-emphasis on demands for high wage increases in favor of more workplace democracy, are all issues capable of realization by traditional means. Strikes, walkouts, sit-ins, and sabotage would undoubtedly bring about changes in our industrial infrastructure more quickly than environmental legislation and any number of health food stores. The Green Ban in Australia, for example, is the name given to the successful refusal of dockworkers and transportation workers to handle environmentally harmful cargo. In fact, the failure of the Green movement to get its message across to ordinary workers and union members has resulted in significant damage to Greens, working people, and the environment.

Further evidence of Bookchin's attempt to distance himself and his theory of social ecology from the mainstream of anarchist thought can be found in his recent book, *The Philosophy of Social Ecology* (1990), in which he attempts to provide a philosophical basis for his social ecological theories. Unfortunately, the rich ecological content of anarchist philosophy is largely un-acknowledged; Bookchin deals only briefly with anarchism's traditional focus on natural models of nonhierarchy and noncentrism. Instead, Bookchin presents us with an intellectual history of the development of social ecological thought, devoting many pages to Diderot's "sensibilities" and Hegel's "concept of spirit" at the expense of Kropotkin's ethical naturalism and

Reclus' bioregionalism—concepts which, at least in the case of Kropotkin, contain important ethical insights that seem to have contributed significantly to the development of Bookchin's own thinking. *The Philosophy of Social Ecology*, subtitled *Essays on Dialectical Naturalism*, directs readers who wish to find out more about the philosophical basis of social ecology and ecological ethics to study the notoriously cloudy pages of Hegel's *Phenomenology of Spirit.*

The reasons for Bookchin's disillusionment with the organized anarchist movement must remain a matter for speculation. A generous explanation of his objectives is that he wishes to produce an ecological alternative that does not scare people off by using the emotionally loaded and popularly misunderstood term, "anarchy," meanwhile integrating into a broadly anti-statist framework the anarchistic ideas floating around in the peace, environmental, and feminist movements. If this is indeed his intention he has, in my opinion, been quite successful. His theory of social ecology is presented in a rational and secular format that permits meaningful dialogue with subscribers to other bodies of thought.

To be fair, Bookchin does acknowledge the influence of anarchist theoretician and geographer Peter Kropotkin in all of the above-mentioned works. However, he does so only in passing, and certainly exhibits no real desire to deal with Kropotkin's thought in the detail that it deserves. The themes with which both Bookchin and Kropotkin deal are, of course, not new; the battles between nature and the profit motive, freedom and tyranny, and liberty and authority, have been with us since the beginning of human society, and neither Bookchin nor Kropotkin originated the anarchist position. Nonetheless, with the important exception of his analysis of the development of patriarchy, all of the basic components of Bookchin's social ecological vision—diversity, decentralization, complementarity, alternative technology, municipal socialism, self-sufficiency, and direct democracy—are found in the works of the great anarchist thinkers of the past. Elisee Reclus and Peter Kropotkin both advocated a global federation of autonomous and ecologically integrated cities and towns; Bookchin has done us the service of updating these ideas and presenting them in modern form.

However, to take all the major ecological insights of anarchist theory and practice and dress them up in a socialist-feminist cum neo-hegelian garb, and then go on to more or less claim them as his own is reprehensible. And to actively misrepresent the movement from which these ideas originally came is an intellectual outrage.

---

1. *Towards an Ecological Society*, by Murray Bookchin. Montreal: Black Rose Books, 1980, pp. 123-126.

2. *The Modern Crisis*, by Murray Bookchin. Montreal: Black Rose Books, ch. 4.

3. *The Modern Crisis*, chapter 4.

Anarchism, Feminism, and the Green Revolution

The Concept of "Home"

According to the Oxford English Dictionary, *eco* is derived from *oikos*, meaning house or home place. Of course, the Greek concept of home can be understood in its broadest sense to mean "vicinity," covering anything from the backyard veggie patch to the entire biosphere. The veggie patch is "home" to a colony of spiders; they, in turn (like it or not), are part of your "home"; and planet Earth is, of course, "home" to all known organic life forms. But in day-to-day life, home is associated with the domestic sphere, the individual household, and, to a lesser extent, the community. It is the place where children are reared and humanity meets its primary needs.

As the anarchist and ecoregional r/evolution progresses, the domestic sphere of life will be increasingly recognized as central to economic and political life. While acknowledging its positive aspects, many Western women (and men) feel that the domestic sphere has become a place of isolation and servitude for women, and that the anarchist r/evolution will, at best, only partially succeed unless domestic work is given respect and social remuneration. Social and cultural emancipation must accompany the liberation of the local economy from the grasps of state and capital, or we will have gained little. Failure to recognize this fact is one important reason why some small-scale communal experiments have so consistently failed to retain female members, upon whom the bulk of domestic responsibilities have usually fallen.

Anarchists have been aware of this issue for generations. The great 19th-century Russian nihilist, anarchist, and bio-geographer,

Peter Kropotkin, understood that the area of domestic work would have to be much more seriously addressed by male anarchists and socialists if a free and equal society was to become a reality. Although some of Kropotkin's ideas about domestic technology and communal organization seem a little odd and old-fashioned today, the spirit of what he said in *The Conquest of Bread* remains relevant:

> A society regenerated by the Revolution will make domestic slavery disappear—this last form of slavery, perhaps the most tenacious, because it is also the most ancient. Only it will not come about in the way dreamt of by Phalansterians [advocates of a type of hierarchically organized socialist community first proposed by Charles Fourier], nor in the manner often imagined by authoritarian Communists. . . .
>
> A phalanstery, which is in fact nothing but an immense hotel, can please some, and even all at a certain period of their life, but the great mass prefers family life (family life of the future, be it understood). . . . Isolation, alternating with time spent in society, is the normal desire of human nature. This is why one of the greatest tortures in prison is the impossibility of isolation, much as solitary confinement becomes torture in its turn, when not alternated with hours of social life.
>
> Other Socialists reject the phalanstery. But when you ask them how domestic work can be organized, they answer: "Each can do 'his own work.' My wife manages the house; the wives of bourgeois will do as much." And if it is a bourgeois playing at Socialism who speaks, he will add, with a gracious smile to his wife: "Is it not true, darling, that you would do without a servant in a Socialist society? You would work like the wife of our good comrade Paul or the wife of John the carpenter?" Servant or wife, man always reckons on woman to do the housework.
>
> But woman, too, at last claims her share in the emancipation of humanity. She no longer wants to be the beast of burden of the house. She considers it sufficient work to give many years of her life to the rearing of her children. She no longer wants to be the cook, the mender, the sweeper of the house! . . .
>
> Households are emerging from their present state of isolation; they begin to associate with other households to do in common what they did separately. In fact, in the future we shall not have a brushing machine, a machine for washing up plates, a third for washing linen, and so on, in each house. "Fifty fires burn," wrote

an American woman the other day, "where one would suffice!" Dine at home, at your own table, with your children, if you like; but only think yourself, why should these fifty women waste their whole morning to prepare a few cups of coffee and a simple meal! Why fifty fires, when two people and one single fire would suffice to cook all these pieces of meat and all these vegetables? Choose your own beef or mutton to be roasted if you are particular. Season the vegetables to your taste if you prefer a particular sauce! But have a single kitchen with a single fire, and organize it as beautifully as you are able to.

Why has woman's work never been of any account? Why in every family are the mother and three or four servants obliged to spend so much time at what pertains to cooking? Because those who want to emancipate mankind have not included woman in their dream of emancipation, and consider it beneath their masculine dignity to think "of those kitchen arrangements," which they have put on the shoulders of that drudge—woman.

To emancipate woman is not only to open the gates of the university, the law courts, or the parliaments to her, for the "emancipated" woman will always throw domestic toil on to another woman. To emancipate woman is to free her from the brutalizing toil of kitchen and washhouse; it is to organize your household in such a way as to enable her to rear her children, if she be so minded, while still retaining sufficient leisure to take her share of social life.

It will come. As we have said, things are already improving. Only let us fully understand that a revolution, intoxicated with the beautiful words, Liberty, Equality, Solidarity, would not be a revolution if it maintained slavery at home. Half of humanity subjected to the slavery of the hearth would still have to rebel against the other half.

In this passage, Kropotkin is responding to Charles Fourier's assertions about the organization of domestic labor, made nearly a century earlier:

[Women are] unproductive because they are absorbed in household work, which entails the wasteful duplication of functions . . . One of the principal savings of the combined order will result from the gathering together of all minor domestic jobs or household tasks.[1]

As Kropotkin points out, though, human beings do not necessarily want to institutionalize social life and its "minor" domestic tasks by, for example, cooking and eating together every day around long tables, as is common in boarding schools and monasteries. In our society at least, most people would probably prefer to have the choice of eating in their own homes or apartments (perhaps through a centrally cooked "take-out" arrangement as was attempted in some early 20th century American experiments), or else at family tables inside communal dining rooms. But the idea that every house should have its own washing machine, large kitchen, fully equipped children's play areas, etc., is not only extremely environmentally destructive, but hugely multiplies the amount of domestic work that needs to be done. Domestic and neighborhood planning and architecture should aim to minimize waste and maximize options for both social interaction and privacy. Community daycare centers, laundry facilities, and vegetable gardens should be located in such a way that, although family and private life will be respected and the private apartment or cottage retained, the self-contained house, crammed full of wasteful appliances, will disappear.

Not much will have changed, though, if only women do the laundry—and for no pay; and it doesn't matter greatly whether they'd do it at home or in communal laundries. This is one place where social anarchists and feminists agree that fundamental cultural change is needed. A truly communal approach to domestic labor requires recognition of the real skills involved in this work, extensive neighborhood cooperation among women (and men), and a much more responsible attitude on the part of men. All facets of domestic management and labor must involve both genders, whether inside individual households, in neighborhood domestic workplaces, or both.[2]

Changes in the management and performance of domestic labor are clearly necessary to the eco/house-revolution. Additionally, maintaining a vegetable patch, participating in the local tree-planting brigade, collecting vegetable wastes, and recycling are new types of "domestic" labor, at least in the West, whose volume is likely to greatly increase as humanity redesigns its towns and cities according to Green principles. Thus, while men should perform their (over)due share of traditional domestic labor and participate equally in communal domestic work, both sexes will share expanded "domestic" duties encompassing community and bioregion—tree planting, gardening, river cleaning, weeding of local woodlands, landscaping, environmental cleanup, etc. The artificial separation between home and social life initiated by the Industrial Revolution will break down; household, community, and bioregion will provide different kinks of opportunities for the intimacy and privacy that we associate with "home."

Women and Anarchism

Anarchism has always attracted a great many intellectually gifted and determined women. One was French communard Louise Michelle (1830–1905), nicknamed the Red Virgin, whose love of nature, women, animals, and liberty dance across every page of her *Memoirs*. The practical steps that she took to help animals, the poor, and her fellow female teachers are still able to inspire us all. Emma Goldman (1869–1940) who, unlike Michelle, was a lover of men, clearly understood that there was a specifically women's politics which had been stifled by the affairs of men and Victorian stuffiness toward sexuality. Emma Goldman worked actively with women in the textile industry, and served several jail terms, including a sentence for "illegally" distributing free condoms and providing information on safe sex and contraception.

Whereas Michelle's writings are scattered and incomplete, convincing us of the righteousness of women's call for liberation largely through her passion, Goldman was a consummate feminist and anarchist thinker whose rational ideas and arguments were presented in a large body of work. Born in a Jewish ghetto in Tsarist Russia in 1869, Goldman began working in a St. Petersburg factory shortly after finishing elementary school, reaching womanhood around the same time as the Nihilist movement was at its height. Coming from an authoritarian and patriarchal family, she was deeply influenced by the Nihilist women, who espoused independence, self-education, and a willingness to give their lives for the ideals they cherished. At the age of 16, Goldman fled to America to avoid the humiliation of an arranged marriage and the narrowness of ghetto life. She converted to anarchism after the 1887 legal murder of the Haymarket martyrs in Chicago, and became a distinguished agitator, activist and writer. Her analysis and criticism of the Suffragist movement has much to say to the middle class wing of today's women's movement; she was sharply critical of the Suffragists, who were, with a few notable exceptions, deeply racist and classist at heart, and merely interested in piecemeal legislative reforms. The legal and economic "freedoms" accorded to women have led, as Goldman prophesized, to the liberation of neither women nor men. Her more general and considered statements about women's emancipation remain as relevant today as they were in her own time:

> The development of woman, her freedom, her independence, must come from and through herself. First, by asserting herself as a personality, and not as a sex commodity. Second, by refusing the right to anyone over her body; by refusing to bear children, unless she wants them; by refusing to be a servant to God, the State, society, the husband, the family, etc., by making her life simpler, but deeper and richer. That is, by trying to learn the meaning and substance of life in all its complexities, by freeing herself from the fear of public opinion and public condemnation. Only that, and not the ballot, will set woman free, will make her a force hitherto unknown in the world, a force for real love, for peace, for harmony; a force of divine fire, of life-giving; a creator of free men and women.[3]

The reason for the interest of women like Louise Michelle and Emma Goldman in anarchism during the 19th and early 20th centuries is not hard to discern. Two centuries ago, Mary Wollstonecraft, the early British feminist and proto-anarchist, wrote at length exposing the tyrannical nature of patriarchy. Her mockery of the pomposity and idiosyncracies of male-dominated domestic and public life underscored the necessity of a multi-faceted attack upon all hierarchical cultural institutions. The following extended passage illustrates the fact that at a very early date discerning thinkers realized that freedom and female emancipation were closely related:

It is vain to expect virtue from women till they are, in some degree, independent of men; nay it is vain to expect that strength of natural affection which would make them good wives and mothers. Whilst they are absolutely dependent on their husbands they will be cunning, mean, and selfish, and the men who can be gratified by the fawning fondness of spaniel-like affection have not much delicacy, for love is not to be bought. . . .

[I]n the education of women, the cultivation of the understanding is always subordinate to the acquirement of some corporeal accomplishment; even while enervated by confinement and false notions of modesty, the body is prevented from attaining that grace and beauty which relaxed half-formed limbs never exhibit. Besides, in youth their faculties are not brought forward by emulation; and having no serious scientific study, if they have natural sagacity it is turned too soon on life and manners. They dwell on effects and modifications, without tracing them back to causes; and complicated rules to adjust behavior are a weak substitute for simple principles. . . .

As a proof that education gives this appearance of weakness to females, we may instance the example of military men, who are, like them, sent into the world before their minds have been stored with knowledge or fortified by principles. The consequences are similar; soldiers acquire a little superficial knowledge, snatched from the muddy current of conversation, and from continually mixing with society, they gain what is termed a knowledge of the world; and this acquaintance with manners and customs has frequently been confounded with punctilious politeness. Where is then the sexual difference when the education has been the same? All the difference that I can discern arises from the superior advantage of liberty, which enables the former to see more of life.[4]

Writing several decades later, the French "utopian" socialist Charles Fourier mounted an unrelenting attack upon patriarchy which concludes by advising women to give up attempting to compete with men in a male world. (Fourier seems curiously unaware of the irony of a male writer, advocating the liberation of women, advising women that they should not compete with men, and, specifically, that they should not bother with "the banal glory of writing books"!) Instead, he advises, women should become "liberators" who will fight the institutions of patriarchy from the outside, and thereby "raise their sex from degradation":

Man already seems to have a premonition of the future; he becomes indignant and alarmed when women belie the prejudice which accuses them of inferiority . . .

Why should women have bothered about the banal glory of writing books, of adding a few volumes to the millions of useless ones already in existence? What women should have produced was not writers but liberators, a political Spartacus, a genius who would devise means of raising their sex from degradation.[5]

Deeply influenced by the writings of Fourier, the Nihilists of 19th century Russia sought to overthrow Tsardom and initiate free federations of ecologically integrated and self-determining peasant villages. The Nihilists were largely composed of middle-class women who had become disgusted with a society which treated them as playthings. Before they were persecuted, imprisoned, exiled, and executed in the thousands–repression which forced them to continue their political activities under-ground–these women exhibited their contempt for Russian society by cutting their hair short and wearing practical working clothes. Peter Kropotkin (fellow Nihilist and, later, geographer and anarchist theoretician) said of the character and outlook of the Nihilist comrades:

Marriage without love, and familiarity without friendship, were equally repudiated. The nihilist girl, compelled by her parents to be a doll in a Doll's House, and to marry for property's sake, preferred to abandon her house and her silk dresses. She put on a black woolen dress of the plainest description, cut off her hair, and went to a high school, in order to win there her personal independence. The woman who saw that her marriage was no longer a marriage, that neither love nor friendship connected those who were legally considered husband and wife, preferred to break a bond which retained none of its essential features. Accordingly she often went with her children to face poverty, prefering loneliness and misery to a life which, under conventional conditions, would have given a perpetual lie to her best self.[6]

Thus, the progressive wing of modern feminism has roots which extend much farther back and much wider than the narrow, middle-class, American suffrage movement; and one of the most important of those roots is anarchism.

Ecology and Eco-Feminism

The near-simultaneous development of the anti-nuclear, peace, women's, and ecology movements has led to the involvement of large numbers of women in Green issues. The fact that women have a history and a culture that is more peaceful than that of men has led to the participation in—and leadership by—large numbers of women in the environmental movement. That women may have come to Green ideas from paths that differ from those taken by men does not, however, support the underlying argument of some eco-feminists—that women have an inborn, "unique" relationship with nature (rather than a learned, cultural tendency toward nurturing behavior). This is an assertion that can never be proven, any more than the assertions that the pope has a special and privileged relationship with God, or that the Jews are "God's chosen people." Each of us experiences nature in our own way, according to the peculiarities of our personalities and individual experiences, and there is no reason to suppose that one's gender is of overriding importance in this respect.

That women have been ill-treated and oppressed under patriarchy is indisputable, and for this reason women as women have had to fight a separate revolution. It is far from complete; there are still many important areas in which women must continue to fight, and men to change. The eco-social anarchist revolution involves issues and demands activity in all areas of life, at least some of which are of no special concern to women. While it is clear that one can be both a feminist and an environmentalist, and that there are in some senses profound points of coincidence between the environmental and feminist movements, eco-feminism alone—because of its relatively narrow focus—cannot form the basis for a durable social and political philosophy.

An attempt has been made to construct such a philosophy along both secular and spiritual lines. The secular version argues, among other things, that because of women's reproductive and nurturant functions, they are more closely related to, and suited to be the guardians of, nature than are men. Although the Earth is undoubtedly in urgent need of nurturing, healing, and repair, the idea of some cultural and eco-feminists that the nurture that a mother bestows on her children makes her *inherently* more capable than men of healing the Earth is biologically reductionist. This is not to say that the *experience* of parenthood does not typically engender a deep appreciation of the natural processes of life-death-birth and renewal, and a generalized life-positive attitude in many women—but such attitudes and appreciations are accessible to nonparents and to men, as well as to mothers.

More generally, the ecological struggle ha the ability to draw people and nature together in a way that no other social and political movement of our time can equal. In its assertion that the male/female division should be considered the most important line of demarcation in nature and society, radical feminism is unhelpful and divisive, setting up battles within an ecology movement that is capable of superseding such useless internecine struggles. Ecology is not primarily concerned with the relationship between humans (men, women, and children) and other life forms. It focuses, rather, upon relationships among all life forms, as well as between biotic (living) things and the abiotic (unliving) environments that they inhabit. Crude, bio-reductionist assertions about female (or male, or racial) superiority serve no good purpose; they only serve to divide the Green movement—and other progressive movements—into antagonistic camps.

An attempt is also underway to promote belief in an inherent woman-nature connection via spiritual imagery: the time-honored metaphor of the Earth Goddess, or Mother Nature. Adherents of this doctrine ask us to believe that the Earth is a goddess—or was created by an actual goddess—to whom homage should be paid. This idea is closely linked with certain New Age philosophies.

The Sydney morning *Herald* recently featured "New Age" (supposedly alternative) bookshops and suppliers in its classified section, the advertisement filling up an entire page. Indeed, we may be sure that many millions of dollars are now made every year through the sale of magic crystals, mystical tracts, Tarot cards, and the like. Astrology, an ancient pseudo-science repopularized in the 1960s, and now very popular in New Age circles, has become a multi-million dollar industry, with an estimated 55 million believers in the U.S. alone. Belief in a Mother Goddess is undoubtedly a byproduct of starry-eyed "New Age" and cultural feminist ideologies, and it's a belief that has, in some cases at least, warped perspectives and seriously undermined serious thinking in both the ecology and feminist movements.

At one time it was possible to laugh off or simply ignore the antics of born-again "Jesus Freaks," astrologers, and spiritual eco-feminists. This is no longer the case, as their ideas have spread like a seemingly unstoppable brush fire within academia and within the radical feminist and ecology movements. The now commonplace acceptance of the questionable premise that astrology "is an organized body of thought capable of ascertaining truth" is evidence enough that New Ageism has already found fertile ground among the populace.

In our emphasis upon replacing capitalism and the totalitarian state with the "free society," anarchists in recent years have forgotten that religious indoctrination and impositions have been every bit as responsible as more secular forces for enslaving human minds and for perpetuating servile attidues toward authority. From the time of Mikhail Bakunin's classical study, *God and the State* (which, interestingly, attacks the scientific academy as being as dangerous as the organized church), to Chaz Bufe's recent pamphlet, *Astrology: Fraud or Superstition?*, anarchists have consistently stressed the idea that the attainment of a free and classless society is dependent upon humankind giving up both government and organized religion. The emergence of religiosity in new and increasingly popular "spiritual" forms in most cases represents a positive threat to the goals and aspirations of the anarchist, feminist, and environmental movements, heralding the onset of another Dark Age, not a New Age.

If this conclusion seems extreme, consider what Chaz Bufe says about religiosity/mysticism (including "New Ageism") in his pamphlet, *Listen Anarchist!* :

> While this may appear to be harmless lunacy, it's not. Rejection of rationality and reversion to mysticism are serious problems. For once you abandon rationality, how do you determine right from wrong? How do you determine what's in your best interest from what isn't? Without rationality you have two choices: you can follow the leader and obey the prescriptions of others; or you can follow your impulses—do what "feels right"—a choice that more often than not leads back to the first.
>
> Using unexamined impulse as a means of decision making is

very dangerous because we've all been subjected to constant authoritarian conditioning since birth, and our impulses will inevitably be influenced to some degree by that conditioning. For example, it obviously "felt right" to a large segment of the German working class to support Hitler during the 1920s and '30s. But was it in their self-interest to do so? Without rationally analyzing the question, how could they have known that what "felt right" to them was absolutely contrary to their own interests? Without rationality there was no way they could have known. Rational thinking was necessary, but they didn't do it. Instead, they goose-stepped into the holocaust with the mystical abstractions of god and fatherland dancing in their heads.

And if anarchists reject rationality and revert to mysticism, it's a safe bet that they too will go goose-stepping off in increasingly authoritarian directions.[7]

It is interesting to note, however, that a secular version of the Mother Earth concept (in which it is understood that the idea is nothing more than a metaphor) has long existed in anarchist literature, harmlessly coevolving alongside rigorously scientific appraisals of the idea of the Earth as a living organism. Elisee Reclus, for example, in his early work, *The Earth*, explored concepts similar to today's Gaia hypothesis. If you were to look for a resolutely secular exegesis of the Earth Mother theme, you would be hard pressed to find a more poetic and well-crafted description of the ancient and time-honored metaphor of the Earth as mother and provider than that given by Reclus. Likewise, it seems no accident that Emma Goldman chose to call her long-running anarchist journal *Mother Earth*, or that Reclus used gender ascription (his/her, mother/father, etc.) when referring to parts of nature.

If women (and men) want to draw inspiration from the Mother Earth metaphor, that's fine. But to confuse myth and literature with philosophy, science, politics, and fact is simply wrong and ultimately dangerous. Literature and philosophy both have their place in our comprehension of natural life processes, but neither Goldman nor Reclus would have tolerated the abject confusion of myth and reality that certain strains of mystical ecology and radical feminism seem determined to promote.

Anarchism, Feminism, and Revolution

The coevolution of the patriarchal family and the state has always been of concern to anarchists. In his influential work, *The Principle of Federation*, 19th-century anarchist thinker P.J. Proudhon analyzed the historical development of the state, concluding that it did not arise from population expansion and military expansion, but was in actual fact the logical extension of the patriarchal family. Modern and genuinely radical feminist thinking on the subject has greatly enriched many anarchists' perceptions of the role of patriarchy in the development of hierarchical state structures. In *The Ecology of Freedom*, Murray Bookchin examines the idea that the emergence of hierarchy and the state resulted from gender inequalities as well as inequalities among men. Although simple differences in age among men (the old dominating the young) contributed to the emergence of hierarchy and eventually the state, anthropologists have documented that it is the appropriation of female-created surplus products in horticultural chiefdoms by old and powerful men, and these same men's need to control paternity and inheritance, that provided the germs of hierarchy. Eventual statism/capitalism, however, is not reducible to male dominance; it is critical to note that only a small percentage of men benefited from high positions in the incipient-state hierarchies. The state—from beginning to end—has destroyed the moral and ecological fabric of the human community; it is, and always has been, a social, economic, and political arrangement based upon raw power, in which the only people to benefit from the destruction of our planet are a handful of powerful men (and, increasingly, a few women).

As Fourier hoped, women have indeed become valiant liberators: Sophia Perovskaya, Louise Michelle, Voltairine de Cleyre, and Emma Goldman, to name but a few. In both her history and character, Louise Michelle is undoubtedly the "female Spartacus" which Fourier foretold; once, wielding a black flag, Michelle successfully rallied the hungry of Paris to grab the bread they needed, by force of numbers alone. Emma Goldman clearly understood that there were many sources of conflict in society and nature other that those between men and women; she knew instinctively and through her own experience that unemployed, immigrant, and working class factory women had little in common with their comfortable, finely dressed, bourgeois sisters.

Even if the middle class wing of the women's movement slowly manages to eliminate the last vestiges of sexual inequality from home, school, factory, legislature, and corporate boardroom, the the state and capitalism will not necessarily disappear; Margaret Thatcher, Indira Gandhi, and others like them have ably adapted to statecraft. Women are now well represented in the bureaucratic classes, and a hierarchy composed equally of women and men at each level would not be much, if any, less totalitarian than a male-dominated hierarchy. Emma Goldman clearly anticipated this situation at the beginning of this century in her controversial essay, "Women's Suffrage":

> Needless to say, I am not opposed to woman suffrage on the conventional ground that she is not equal to it. I see neither physical, psychological, nor mental reasons why woman should not have the equal right to vote with man. But that cannot possibly blind me to the absurd notion that woman will accomplish that wherein man has failed. . . . To assume . . . that she would succeed in purifying something which is not susceptible to purification is to credit her with supernatural powers. . . . Women who are at all conversant with the process of politics, know the nature of the beast, but in their self-sufficiency and egotism they make themselves believe that they have but to pet the beast, and he will become as gentle as a lamb, sweet and pure. As if women have not sold their votes, as if women politicians cannot be bought? . . .
>
> The American suffrage movement has been, until very recently, altogether a parlor affair, absolutely detached from the economic needs of the people. Thus Susan B. Anthony, no doubt an exceptional type of woman, was not only indifferent but antagonistic to labor; nor did she hesitate to manifest her antagonism when, in 1869, she advised women to take the places of striking printers in New York. I do not know whether her attitude had changed before her death.
>
> There are, of course, some suffragists who are affiliated with working women—The Women's Trade Union League, for instance; but they are a small minority, and their activities are essentially economic. The rest look upon toil as a just provision of Providence. What would become of the rich, if not for the poor?

What would become of these idle, parasitic ladies, who squander more in a week than their victims earn in a year, if not for the eighty million wage workers? . . .

Few countries have produced such arrogance and snobbishness as America. Particularly is this true of the American woman of the middle class. She not only considers herself the equal of man, but his superior, expecially in her purity, goodness, and morality. Small wonder that the American suffragist claims for her vote the most miraculous powers. In her exalted conceit she does not see how truly enslaved she is, not so much by man, as by her own silly notions and traditions. Suffrage cannot ameliorate that sad fact; it can only accentuate it, as indeed it does.[8]

To be fair, the labor and the women's movements have been morally blind to each other. The early labor movement was indifferent to women at best, and hostile or patronizing to them at worst; and both movements tended, with notable exceptions, such as the IWW, to be racist as well.

Today's women's movement is clearly not reducible to the radical/separatist and middle-class branches of feminism. Women outside of these groups are increasingly raising the very points that Goldman did: that "women" is not a homogeneous category, and that women differ in class, race, ethnicity, location, motherhood status, and age. Further, most serious feminists who argue that there are postivie aspects of "women's culture" do so on grounds of culture and learning, not biology. Not all women, not even most, share the priority of "equal work for equal pay" so dear to the middle-class women's movement (which is not to say that it's unimportant—just that it's one of *many* issues); instead, issues of health, nutrition, safety, and survival loom large for working class and low income women around the world, including those who consciously unite around "women's" causes.

Authoritarian institutions create authoritarian people—people who wish to boss other people around, or who seek to manipulate and exploit nature and their fellow human beings for their own benefit. The battle is not only, or even mainly, between men and women, but between authoritarians and egalitarians. While we allow massive power structures such as multinational corporations and national governments to dominate society, we can never achieve a free and ecologically balanced system for either gender.

To paraphrase Murray Bookchin, it is the political, social, and economic culture of domination, upheld and perpetuated by the institutions of statism/capitalism, which is the real enemy.

The state, capitalism, and patriarchy together promote an evil, life-negating system based upon individual wealth, power, and prestige at the expense of all life on the planet; they may well destroy so much of nature that the ecosystem will become unable to sustain life in the cycles of reproduction and evolution required for its continued existence. Nowhere is this more evident than in state attitudes toward human sexuality. In the past, classic patriarchal states permitted (indeed, fostered) the rise of ascetically oriented, life-denying fundamentalist theocracies based upon narrow and self-interested versions of Hinduism, Islam, Judaism, or Christianity. Such systems were (and are) characterized by a twin denial of human sexual freedom and the humanity of women (and non-dominant men). Not coincidentally, they almost invariably display a "rape and ruin" attitude toward nature as well. Wilhelm Reich's writings on the suppression of healthy sexual attitudes during the rise of fascism early in this century clearly demonstrate the horrors of the "sexless" (in actuality, anti-sexual and anti-female) modern state.

Today, the patriarchal state remains a monstrous institution with the ability to unleash perhaps irreparable damage upon the social, ecological, and moral fabric of human society. Unless dismantled, it will relentlessly pursue its logic of domination, exploitation, and destruction. Neither men nor women will ever achieve their full potential while statism/capitalism, in inextricable embrace with patriarchy, remain dominant forces.

It is no accident that the two greatest anarchist writers and thinkers of the 19th century, Reclus and Kropotkin, were both professional geographers, who glimpsed that the future of our planet lay not with the nation state but with a global federation of (more or less) self-sustaining communities, ecologically integrated with surrounding bioregions. These 19th century anarchists augued their case in terms of both social justice and ecology. This fact is overlooked by derivative movements such as deep ecology and some branches of the ecofeminist, peace, unionist, animal rights, and antiwar movements. For many years, anarchists have been devising ways to overcome statism/

capitalism; today's environmentalists and feminists would do well to pay closer attention to the ideas, successes, and failures of their anarchist predecessors (and contemporaries).

If it is to succeed, the anarchist eco-social r/evolution will require the combined forces of all social movements concerned with justice. Oppression is multi-faceted; combatting its many aspects requires broadened consciousness and a multitude of interacting solutions. The oppressor's solution to the disorganized protests of the oppressed has always been to unleash the centralized might of state violence and legal repression. Unless oppressed groups stop blathering about passing new laws on this or that issue, and instead realistically admit that the various forms of oppression will continue as long as we pay homage to the institutions of capital and state, no significant change will be possible. Our species must overcome the barriers of greed, prejudice and ignorance. Anarchists, in their relentless quest for justice, equality, and harmony among all living things, applaud every small step that we make toward eliminating narrow self-interest. As two important movements concerned with justice and ecology, feminism and environmentalism will, if they are to succeed, converge into an anarchist quest—whether that quest be known to them as "anarchy" or not.

---

1. Quoted in *The Utopian Vision of Charles Fourier: Selected Texts on Work, Love and Passionate Attraction.* London: Jonathan Cape, 1971, pp. 130-131.

2. See *Redesigning the American Dream: The Future of Housing, Work, and Family Life,* by Dolores Hayden. New York: W.W. Norton & Co.

3. *The Traffic in Women and Other Essays on Feminism.* Seattle: Times Change Press, 1970, p. 63.

4. *A Vindication of the Rights of Women.*

5. Fourier, op. cit.

6. *Memoirs of a Revolutionist*

7. *Listen Anarchist!,* by Chaz Bufe. Tucson, Arizona: See Sharp Press, 1992, pp. 19-20.

8. *The Traffic in Women and Other Essays on Feminism,* pp. 53-61.

Anarchism & Animal Rights

For over a century anarchists have debated the question of human-animal relations. It's thus worth taking the time to examine the ideas and arguments of the 19th century anarchist-vegetarians in some detail.

Toward the end of his life, French social geographer Elisee Reclus published his thoughts on the topic in a short article titled, "On Vegetarianism." Although he insists that his early childhood experiences did not influence his views on the evils of animal husbandry and meat eating, Reclus begins his short study by outlining his innate feelings of disgust for what he considered to be barbaric, retrograde practices:

> First of all, I should say that my search for truth had nothing to do with the early impressions which made me a potential vegetarian while still a small boy. I have a distinct remembrance of horror at the sight of blood. One of the family had sent me, plate in hand, to the village butcher, with the injunction to bring back some gory fragment. In all innocence I set out cheerfully to do as I was bid, and entered the yard where the slaughtermen were. I still remember this gloomy yard where terrifying men went to and fro with great knives, which they wiped on blood-besprinkled smocks. Hanging from a porch an enormous carcass seemed to me to occupy an extraordinary amount of space; from its white flesh a reddish liquid was trickling into the gutters. Trembling and silent I stood in this blood-stained yard, incapable of going forward and much too terrified to run away. I do not know what happened to me; it has passed from my memory. I seem to have heard that I fainted, and that the kind-hearted butcher carried me into his own house; I did not weigh more than one of those lambs he slaughtered every morning.

Reclus found "man's" attempts to interfere with and improve upon nature a particularly disturbing aspect of 19th-century European culture. He argued that such domination resulted in part from a prehistoric change during which "man" the hunter-gatherer stopped respecting the integrity of nature and turned to animal husbandry, thereby interrupting the natural evolution of animal life. As his domination over nonhuman life increased and "man" began to actively select and breed domestic animals, wilderness came to be perceived as an increasingly dangerous place inhabited by wild, predatory beasts.

Absurd attempts by "packs of engineers" to "improve" a valley could, Reclus claimed, be directly related to "man's" attempt to achieve domination over our animal relatives:

> It is one of the sorriest results of our flesh-eating habits that the animals sacrificed to man's appetite have been systematically and methodically made hideous, shapeless, and debased in intelligence and moral worth. The name even of the animal into which the boar has been transformed is used as the grossest of insults; the mass of flesh we see wallowing in noisome pools is so loathsome to look at that we agree to avoid all similarity of name between the beast and the dishes we make out of it. . . . A similar degradation has befallen the ox, which nowadays we see moving with difficulty in the pastures, transformed by stock-breeders into an enormous ambulating mass of geometrical forms, as if designed beforehand for the knife of the butcher. And it is to the reproduction of such monstrosities we apply the term "breeding!" This is how man fulfills his mission as educator with respect to his brethren, the animals.

> For that matter, do we not act in like manner towards all Nature? Turn loose a pack of engineers into a charming valley, in the midst of fields and trees, or on the banks of some beautiful river, and you will soon see what they would do. They would do everything in their power to put their own work in evidence, and to mask Nature under their heaps of broken stones and coal. All of them would be proud, at the least, to see their locomotives streaking the sky with a trail of dirty yellow or black smoke.

> In a similar spirit the butchers display before the eyes of the public, even in the most frequented streets, disjointed carcasses, gory chunks of meat, and think to placate our aesthetic senses by boldly decorating the flesh they dole out with garlands of roses!

Reclus did not hesitate to link meat eating, violence, and warfare, concluding that despite the macho mythology connecting meat eating, strength, and vigor, the physical condition of meat eaters could not match the health, endurance, and inner strength of people with temperate eating habits:

> It is not a digression to mention the horrors of war in connection with the massacre of cattle and carnivorous banquets. The diet of individuals corresponds closely to their manners. Blood demands blood. On this point anyone who searches among his recollections of the people whom he has known will find there can be no possible doubt as to the contrast which exists between vegetarians and coarse eaters of flesh, greedy drinkers of blood, in amenity of manner, gentleness of disposition, and regularity of life. . . .
> According to [meat-eaters], mildness signifies feebleness: the sick are only in the way, and it would be a charity to get rid of them. If they are not killed, they should at least be allowed to die. But it is just these delicate people who resist disease better than the robust. Full-blooded and high-coloured men are not always those who live longest: the really strong are not necessarily those who carry their strength on the surface, in a ruddy complexion, distended muscle, or a sleek and oily stoutness.

Questions of health, ecology, taste, or morals, however, pale before the real issue at stake in humanity's relationship with the animals: whether we will ever enter into a more natural co-evolution with all other living, evolving things:

> For the great majority of vegetarians, the question is not whether their biceps and triceps are more solid than those of the flesh-eaters, nor whether their body is better able to resist the risks of life and the chances of death . . . For them the important point is the recognition of the bond of affection and goodwill that links man to the so-called lower animals, and the extension to these our brothers of the sentiment which has already put a stop to cannibalism among men. The reasons which might be pleaded by anthropophagists against the disuse of human flesh in their customary diet would be as well-founded as those urged by ordinary flesh-eaters today. The arguments that were opposed to that monstrous habit [cannibalism] are precisely those we

vegetarians employ now. The horse and the cow, the rabbit and the capon, the deer and the hare, the pheasant and the lark, please us better as friends than as meat. We wish to preserve them either as respected fellow workers, or simply as companions in the joy of life and friendship.

Reclus did not trivialize the age-old philosophical contradiction between the vegetarian ideal and other human-nature inter-actions: If animals should be spared, why not also trees and bacterial life? In a letter written around 1890, Reclus was hesitant about taking his principles to extreme lengths, arguing that the liberation of humanity from state and capital would have to take place before liberation could be achieved for the vast majority of men, women, children and animals.

> But, so you asked me: "Do you exclude the animals?" This is certainly a weighty question. . . . For my part, I embrace also the animals in my affection of socialist solidarity. But I also say to myself: Everything is accomplished by degrees and the first duties begin around us. Let us realize justice in the largest circle we can, first in the civilized circle, then in the human circle. Each realization of a partial ideal will make us more sensible, more delicate for the future realization of a larger ideal. . . . My firm confidence has it that our harmonious society must embrace not only men, but all beings conscious of their lives. Where is the limit? I don't know this, I only know that, it is beyond the animals killed to shoe us and to supply butcher's meat.[1]

By the time he wrote "On Vegetarianism" in 1901, Reclus had clarified his views on the relationship between human health, animal freedom, and free coevolution. First, vegetarians should be tolerant of meat-eaters, but the latter should have the common decency to at least hide the more bloodthirsty aspects of their habit from general view. Second, Reclus never embraced the more radical "veganist" position (not only no meat, but no eggs or dairy products), and concludes his essay with a charming piece of French philosophical gastronomy that will alarm cholesterol worriers, but may yet prove to be true:

One thing is certain, that if we . . . [push] the practice of our
theory to its ultimate and logical consequences. . . we should fall
into simple absurdity. . . . It is clear that we have no intention of
subordinating all our practices and actions . . . to a respect for the
life of the infinitely little; we shall not let ourselves die of hunger
and thirst, like some Buddhist, when the microscope has shown us
a drop of water swarming with animalculae. We shall not hesitate
now and then to cut ourselves a stick in the forest, or to pick a
flower in a garden; we shall even go so far as to take a lettuce, or
cut cabbages and asparagus for our food, although we fully
recognise the life in the plant as well as in animals. But it is not
for us to found a new religion, and to hamper ourselves with a
sectarian dogma; it is a question of making our existence as
beautiful as possible, and in harmony, so far as in us lies, with the
aesthetic conditions of our surroundings.

We want some day to live in a city where we shall no longer see
butchers' shops full of dead bodies side by side with drapers' or
jewellers', and facing a druggist's, or hard by a window filled with
choice fruits, or with beautiful books, engravings or statuettes, and
works of art. We want an environment pleasant to the eye and in
harmony with beauty. . . .

What then are the foods which seem to correspond better with
our ideal of beauty both in their nature and in their needful
methods of preparation? They are precisely those which from all
time have been appreciated by men of simple life; the foods which
can do best without the lying artifices of the kitchen. They are
eggs, grains, fruits. . . . Man gets them for his food without killing
the being that provides them, since they are formed at the point
of contact between two generations. Do not our men of science
who study organic chemistry tell us, too, that the egg of the animal
or plant is the best storehouse of every vital element?

It should be noted that the prominent use of the word "man"
throughout Reclus' writing seems at first sight to be old-fashioned
and straightforwardly sexist. Upon closer inspection, however, one
finds his use of gender ascription is complex, sensitive, and highly
relevant to recent discussions among feminists, anarchists, and
animal rightists. That is, his comments on interspecies
relationships are a provocative indictment of what is more
typically "man's," rather than "woman's," treatment of our non-
human companions (at least in the West):

One of my strongest impressions of my childhood is that of having witnessed one of those rural dramas, the forcible killing of a pig by a party of villagers in revolt against a dear old woman who would not consent to the murder of her fat friend. The village crowd burst into the pigsty and dragged the beast to the slaughter place where all the apparatus for the deed stood waiting, whilst the unhappy dame sat down upon a stool weeping quiet tears. I stood beside her and saw those tears without knowing whether I should sympathise with her grief, or think with the crowd that the killing of the pig was just, legitimate, decreed by common sense as well as by destiny.[2]

Louise Michelle, a communard like Reclus and a lifelong friend of Kropotkin, was famous for her concern about animals. Like Reclus, Michelle was a lifelong vegetarian, a believer in scientific progress, and vehemently opposed to animal experimentation. Her words anticipate the contemporary animal rights movement as well as the development of vitamin-enriched supplements as alternatives to meat:

As far back as I can remember, the origin of my revolt against the powerful was my horror at the tortures inflicted on animals. I used to wish animals could get revenge, that the dog could bite the man who was mercilessly beating him, that the horse bleeding under the whip could throw off the man tormenting him. But mute animals always submit to their fate . . . and the more ferocious a man is toward animals, the more that man cringes before the people who dominate him. . . .

I was accused of allowing my concern for animals to outweigh the problems of humans [during the Paris Commune uprising in 1871] when I ran to help a cat in peril. . . . The unfortunate beast was crouched in a corner that was being scoured by shells, and it was crying out like a human being. . . .Why should I be so sad over brutes, when reasoning beings are so unhappy? The answer is that everything fits together, from the bird whose brood is crushed to the humans whose nests are destroyed by war. . . .

Even in a gutter like a laboratory, a beast is sensitive both to caresses and to brutalities. More often it feels brutalities. People find it interesting to torture a poor animal to study mechanisms which are already well known. . . .

I dream of the time when science will give everyone enough to eat. Instead of the putrefied flesh which we are accustomed to eating, perhaps science will give us chemical mixtures containing more iron and nutrients than the blood and meat we now absorb. The first bite might not flatter the palate as much as the food we now eat, but it will not be . . . rotten, and it will build stronger and purer bodies for men weakened by generations of famine or the excesses of their ancestors.[3]

Beyond the question of whether animals or their products should be eaten or utilized is the extreme notion that animals should never be used by humanity for any purpose whatsoever. Although we all want to preserve the free mustang and the wild buffalo, the intelligent and humane use of already domesticated animals such as horses, draft cattle, and many others, could do much to improve the environment. In Thailand, for instance, the use of mechanical vehicles has led to a worrying decline in the traditional use of elephants, and the forest is suffering as a result. In Australia, bullock trains were the traditional method of moving logs before the arrival of the bulldozer and semi truck. In British Columbia, the use of heavy horses to gently extract selectively harvested timber from forests under sustainable management practices shows us a way to move logs without constructing roads or flattening the forest. The reintroduction of horses, elephants, and bullocks on farms and in forests could allow us to sustainably manage forest and transport agricultural products in a pollution-free, low impact manner.

Donkeys, horses, cattle, and oxen were the most common method of human transportation within cities before the dominance of the motor car. (In our modern city, things have become so congested that cars often move no faster than donkeys, let alone horses!) In the 19th century, manure was collected from the streets and stables of Paris and shipped by barge to adjoining country districts. It was then used by gardeners, by means of hot-house horticulture in raised beds, to organically produce most of the city's winter vegetables. Needless to say, fresh vegebales and the exhilarating experience of horseback riding are infinitely preferable to smog and drive-through fast food outlets.

Carrier pigeons can also be used as an effective and cost-saving transport system. At the blood testing center at Cotentin, France, pigeons have been used for many years to transport blood samples from outlying hospitals. In rural and mountainous regions, the use of pigeons for transport would be much quicker and far less costly than the use of roads and motor vehicles. There is no reason why pigeons, currently considered a pest in many cities of the world, could not be utilized as part of city-wide postage and message systems. They live for up to 20 years and are almost entirely reliable. Their droppings, which now destroy the embellishments on old and treasured buildings in many cities, could be contained to a great extent in dovecotes, and could be used as manure in urban and community gardens.

In the past, barn owls were encouraged to nest in specially constructed farm buildings in many parts of Europe in order to control mice. In Malaysia, this system has been successfully reintroduced, and the number of barn owls there has doubled in recent years.

In the past, many animals were welcomed into our fields, farms, and homes because of the useful services they performed for us. Cats and dogs have been used by humans to control pests and to guard our houses for thousands of years; the relationship between people and their cats and dogs is often one of love and symbiosis, not of cruelty and exploitation.

But today, traditional breeds of shire horses are kept alive only by enthusiasts. Barn owls are absent in many places because of the past use of DDT and the present use of other chemical poisons to control mice, all of which poison the owls who eat them. And the few remaining working elephants are given to circuses where they are shame-lessly displayed in sideshows, or else they are considered economically redundant and uselessly slaughtered. Thus, thousands of years of careful horse breeding, the art of elephant husbandry, and the beautiful sight of the barn own at twilight are all threatened by the tractor, the earth-mover, and the indiscriminate application of inorganic chemicals. Even if we do not wish to exploit animals for their meat, increasing the humane employment of animals would not only improve the environment but lead to a more fulfilling relationship with many creatures once considered vital to human life.

The questions of vegetarianism and animal rights are far from new to anarchists. While the ethical arguments against both meat eating and, especially, animal experimentation seem convincing, the ecological arguments against the humane use of animals and against meat eating seem, upon examination, to be far less so. This final argument (against meat eating) is taken up in a separate essay. [See next essay—Ed.]

---

1. *Elisee and Elit Reclus: In Memoriam,* Joseph Ishill, ed. "Letter to Richard Heath."

2. "On Vegetarianism."

3. *Memoirs,* by Louise Michelle. University of Alabama Press, 1981, pp. 24-30.

Microlivestock, Economy,
and Ecology

Anarcho-environmentalists often promote vegetarianism, or at least call for minimizing the consumption of large livestock, on the grounds that we must stop eating so high on the food chain. Not to do so, they argue, channels too much grain to meat production (it takes seven pounds of grain to produce one pound of beef) and damages the land through overgrazing. Thus many environmentalists, vegetarians, and vegans assert that livestock raising should be abandoned altogether.

The call to give up animal husbandry and to grow more beans and grains is only valid, however, where the land is suitable for *permanent* cultivation. Only a small percentage of the Earth's surface is arable, and even much of this area cannot be sustainably cultivated on a permanent basis. Approximately 70% of available land in developing countries is marginal or forested, and is useful solely as a source of animal forage. Livestock can process forage and inedible (to humans) waste-crop materials into food sources (meat, milk, and eggs) with high vitamin and protein content. Beyond this, livestock produce a wide range of extremely valuable byproducts. Dung is a fertilizer, soil stabilizer, and prized fuel source in areas where timber is scarce. Hides, wool, fur, and feathers are often more valuable than milk, eggs, or meat. Also, many animals, including pigeons, ducks, and geese, feed themselves by scavenging, and in the process are much more effective in controlling weed and insect populations than are conventional chemical spraying and furrowing procedures.

Meat eating is unlikely to disappear in the near future; nor is the continued hunting of wild game animals likely to be effectively controlled by government enforcement agencies. The tragic failure of efforts to prevent the poaching of rhinos and

tigers in Africa, Asia, India, and China points to this fact. In New
Guinea, for example, the overhunting of wild game has led to a
significant decline in numbers of once-common native animals.
There the introduction of the domestic rabbit at the village level
is seen by many people as an answer to this problem. Domestic
rabbits (unlike the wild species which have devastated Australia)
cannot survive in the wild and are not invasive. They can be easily
reared in small enclosures and fed on clover, thus providing fresh
meat for the villagers while lessening the demand upon native
animals.

It is a matter of fact that many cultures consume wild animals as
an integrated part of their cultural systems. Although we may wish
to discourage meat eating, it is unlikely that habits will change
quickly enough to avoid extinction of many species of the larger
game animals. If we are to conserve animals and rainforests, as
well as provide people living on marginal land with an adequate
diet, then the adoption of animal husbandry using indigenous
and non-conventional livestock is absolutely essential. Small
antelope, rodents, iguanas, jungle fowl, and other small native
species have been hunted for generations in many parts of the
world; they typically thrive in areas which are completely
unsuitable for conventional livestock or agriculture. If animals
such as these could be ranched on a free-ranging basis in existing
forests and savannahs, native fruits, tubers, herbs, and fungi
would be preserved in the process.

Factory farming, feed lots, and animal testing, on the other
hand, involve both cruel and environmentally damaging practices
that have no place in any society, let alone an anarchist one.
Despite the fact that, for instance, in East Anglia (England) the
straw and droppings from large-scale chicken farms are now being
combusted in small-scale electricity generating stations, the
excrement produced by lot-fed pigs and cattle continues to be a
real hazard and a major pollutant of British waterways. Although
sewage lagoons and worm farming can effectively and pro-
ductively deal with these wastes, the conditions under which lot-
fed animals are kept offends the sensibilities of even the most
committed carnivore. Finally, the excesses of scientific experi-
mentalism are far too ghastly for almost anyone to endure. I
cannot bear to even open an anti-vivisection pamphlet, as the

pictures are simply too distressing. We should continue to protest these outrages, loudly and resolutely, since such practives horribly degrade both animal and human dignity alike.

Animal and plant life have co-evolved for millions of years; the establishment of integrated permacultural systems in which animals are integrated with crops, forestry or aquaculture is absolutely essential for increasing the overall health and productivity of the land. Thus, while vegetarianism may be desirable in terms of our ethical relationship to other living things, from an ecological viewpoint the arguments for it are far from compelling.

The Advantages of Microlivestock

One reason why vegetarianism as a solution to the world's environmental problems has gained currency in recent years is that agriculturists have focused upon breeding bigger and bigger cattle. They have almost universally failed to study improvements in the gene pool of naturally occurring smaller species, or "microlivestock." (The term "microlivestock" refers to small, edible animals such as rabbits and ducks, and smaller-than-normal versions of game and farm animals, for example, "micropigs" and "microcattle.")

At present confined mainly to certain rural pockets in the Third World, where they are often critical to poor families' survival, microlivestock could become valuable food and animal byproduct resources for all. The advantages of raising microlivestock are myriad: they are less expensive; they are less risky to buy and maintain (if a large cow dies, it is a much greater loss than if a small one dies); they give a faster return through their higher reproductive rates; it's relatively easy to match herd size to available feed; they can eat feed unsuitable for humans or larger livestock; in some cases, they are more efficient converters of food than "normal" livestock; in areas without refregeration, smaller animals come in a readily consumed package; women and children, as well as men, can easily handle them; they generally need little veterinary care; and they require comparatively little space for feeding and handling.

In general, through utilizing smaller animals, humanity could dramatically expand its food base and decrease negative human impact on the environment. As noted above, many livestock can be raised on feeds that humans generally discard or ignore, while others collect minute amounts of feed that would otherwise go unused. For example, chickens and pigeons gather scattered seeds, turkeys and muscovies [ducks] gobble up insects, geese graze weeds, iguana feed in the tops of trees, antelope browse tree leaves, and capybara and grasscutters [large Ghanaian rodents] eat reeds that are not eaten by cattle. Most importantly, small breeds have often evolved by adapting to extremely harsh environments, and can flourish in areas usually deemed completely unsuitable for the raising of livestock. And microlivestock are potentially important for urban areas; if more people utilized small plots of urban land for integrated animal/plant systems, we could substantially reduce the degradation of surrounding rural lands and relieve urban poverty and malnutrition worldwide.

Microbreeds of Cattle, Goats, Sheep, and Pigs

Although microcattle generally produce only modest amounts of milk, manure, hides, blood, horn, bone and meat per animal, the higher head count allows a herd to outyield genetically "improved" larger animals on a per acre basis. Under stressful conditions, the ability of microcattle to survive adversity makes them by far the most efficient kind of cattle. They tend to be active, economical, and agile in tight spaces, and are becoming more common as draft animals in small fields, terraces, and paddies. The small hill cattle of Nepal, for example, are valued because they can negotiate the steep slopes and narrow terraces of the Himalayas. The small hoof size and body weight of such microcattle also means that they cause much less soil damage than conventional breeds. Under hot and humid conditions, they suffer less than larger cattle because of their greater ratio of skin area to body mass. And, unlike larger varieties, microcattle have little or no difficulties in calving. Finally, many microcattle are remarkably resistant to disease. Some breeds in Africa are resistant to trypanosomiasis, an indigenous parasite that makes large areas of the continent uninhabitable for cattle. The Dwarf West African Shorthorn, weighing less than 100 kg, is perhaps the smallest of all cattle, and can be found thriving in the worst disease-infested areas. The smallest cows are now only 60 centimeters tall, and can easily share the barnyard with poultry.

Although they are often disparaged for destroying vegetation on overgrazed lands, small goats provide excellent meat and milk. The Angora and Cashmere goats, often weighing less that 30 kg, produce some of the finest and most valued fibers in the world.

Although sheep weighing less than 35 kg have been largely ignored, such microsheep could boost meat, milk, skin, wool, and pelt production in many villages and small farms in Africa, Asia and Latin America. They are adapted to poor feeds and can graze in wastelands unsuited to any other livestock except less desirable animals such as goats and camels. Microsheep can graze rough grasses that are unpalatable to cattle, and have grazing habits that complement those of goats. With their lesser dietary needs, microsheep can fatten in areas in which the forage preferred by larger breeds is so scattered that the latter cannot cover enough ground in one day to survive. Many breeds reproduce year-round, which allows for the continuous production of premium meat. Microsheep cause little erosion, even on steep slopes or on heavily trampled paths to and around water holes; in South Asia, they have been continuously stocked on the same ground for thousands of years without causing any apparent harm. The Navajo sheep, which comes from a much more arid area of Spain than does the Marino, was first introduced into North America in 1540. Weighing less than 30 kg when mature, the Navajo sheep was once widely raised throughout the American Southwest, and has recently been pulled from the brink of extinction. Its unique wool makes beautiful rugs; it can exist in the most arid deserts without supplementary food and with very little water; and it can successfully raise lambs in searing heat. The small Soay sheep is used in Cornwall, England to graze banks of highly erodible china-clay soil too unstable for heavier animals. Microsheep are also used in some places, rather than expensive chemical defoliants, to prevent brush from smothering newly planted trees; and the lambs from microsheep bring in useful income. Finally, in Malaysia, the sheep population has doubled as farmers have begun grazing microsheep between the trees in rubber plantations.

Most pig breeds are too large to be considered microlivestock, but there are some whose mature weight is less than 70 kg. The Mexican cuino and the pygmy hog of Assam, both of which are endangered, can weigh less than 10 kg, with a shoulder height of 25 cm. Pigs complement other grazing livestock, and eat small roots, leafy trash, or bitter fruits that are not consumed by humans or ruminants. Pigs work well in multiple-cropping schemes and are used in some places to help clear small plots by uprooting weeds, shrubs, and small trees. Vietnamese potbellied pigs are often raised as indoor livestock in Vietnamese cities. They do not get fleas, don't shed hair, and, as a non-rooting breed, are easily house trained. Although in recent years they have become popular, if expensive, house pets in the U.S., their real potential lies in Third World villages and in urban livestock raising, where their non-rooting habits are desirable.

In Southeast Asia, pigs are often raised in conjunction with aquaculture, their manure providing nutrition for edible aquatic plants as well as for fish. Barns are constructed on stilts over lakes, so that animal feces fall into the water. Floating aquatic duckweed (a very nutritious food) thrives on these wastes and can then be fed to the animals. At Louisiana State University, duckweed is being grown in dairy farm wastewater and substituted for alfalfa in dairy and pig feed. The potential for using duckweed to raise fish, poultry, and waterfowl exists in many parts of the world.

In many parts of Southeast Asia, pig and other animal manure is washed into lagoons stocked with fish such as carp or tilapia, and in which water spinach thrives. The fish can then be eaten by humans, and the water spinach fed to the animals. The potential for the integration of fish, animal, and vegetable production is thus very great. Combined with the intelligent use of aquaculture, integrated animal/plant systems can continually produce several crops in the same space, without the addition of imported fertilizers and foodstuffs.

Poultry

The quintessential microlivestock, poultry are common throughout the developing world in both rural and urban settings—and the small scavenger chicken is by far the most common kind of poultry. Bred for temperate climates, North American chickens are highly susceptible to heat, humidity and disease; their smaller jungle counterparts, found in many parts of the Asian and African continents, could be crossbred with the North American chicken to develop new strains resistant to many diseases and pests. (Of the 50 or so breeds which were once common in the West, only two are now raised for meat production.) A common feature of most Third World villages, scavenger chickens are usually self-reliant, hardy birds capable of withstanding the abuses of a harsh climate, minimal management, and inadequate nutrition. They live largely on weed seeds, insects, and kitchen wastes that would otherwise be unused. Such free-ranging chickens are also well suited to urban farming, although their habit of scratching up the soil requires that they be kept out of areas with young seedlings. Specific indigenous feeding practices vary considerably. In Ghana, for example, farmers "culture" termites for poultry consumption by placing a moist piece of cow dung (under a tin) over a known termite nest. The termites burrow into the dung, and some can then be fed to the chickens each day. Because termites can digest cellulose, this system converts waste vegetation into meat.

Though they are a major resource in Asia, domestic ducks are not yet common elsewhere. Most breeds do not require water in which to swim, adapt readily to a wide range of conditions (including small urban farms, where they produce excellent fertilizer), are more resistant to diseases, and are more adept foragers than chickens. Tropical varieties have much lower levels of fat than do traditional farm ducks, and are among the most efficient of all food producers. Apart from their eggs, which are larger and superior to those of chickens, their feathers and down are widely used as a filler for pillows. Ducks have a special fondness for mosquito and beetle larvae, grasshoppers, snails, slugs and crustaceans. Ducks clear fields of scattered grain, rice paddies of burrowing crabs, and remove aquatic weeds and algae from small lakes, ponds, and canals. This not only improves conditions for aquaculture, but produces plump ducks as well.

Although capable of wreaking considerable damage to garden crops, muscovies will eat grass and can tolerate a much wider diet than other ducks. If used more widely, muscovies could contribute much to poor people's food supplies. They provide large quantities of premium quality meat containing little fat, are prolific layers and attentive mothers, and can tolerate extremes of heat and cold. Muscovies are particularly fond of insects; they have been used for a long time to manage fly problems on Canadian farms. One duck placed in a cage containing 100 flies can eat 90 of them within 30 minutes. It takes flypaper, traps, and baits anywhere from 15 to 86 hours to suppress fly populations that much; further, such fly-catching devices are expensive and generally have to be kept away from livestock.

Although very well-suited to marshy areas, geese can thrive away from water, and they are the only domestic fowl that can live and reproduce on a diet consisting solely of grass. They are, however, even more underutilized than ducks. They not only provide meat, but their fat can be rendered into a long-lasting cooking oil, their large eggs are very good to eat, and their down is a fine natural insulating material. Their long necks make them adept at gleaning weeds from hard-to-reach places, such as fence rows and ditches, that frustrate larger livestock. Because geese relish grasses and shun most broad-leafed plants, they have been used extensively in the U.S. to rid cotton fields of grassy weeds. In fact, geese could be used to weed nearly all broad-leafed crops— asparagus, potatoes, berry fruits, mint, grapes, beets, beans, hops, onions, and strawberries. In the past, geese were used in vineyards and fruit orchards to eat both weeds and fallen fruits, which could harbor diseases and parasites. The forest and flower industries could gain much from using these birds for weed control. Goslings can also be used to consume the suckers on corn. Ten geese can clear as many weeds in the same amount of time as a farmer with a hoe; they also fertilize the fields, provide additional income, and work rain, shine, and overtime on moonlit nights.

Similar to pheasants, Guinea fowl require little water (obtaining their moisture from dew), reproduce well in both cool and hot conditions, and retain many of their wild ancestors' survival characteristics. They grow quickly and produce twice as many eggs as do chickens. They are excellent scavengers with a particular love for ant eggs, for which they will open ant hills. Apart from providing eggs and meat, guinea fowl can be used to control insect pests on vegetable crops. In parts of Australia's Queensland, many farmers keep them to control grasshoppers and ticks in and around cattle yards. The birds do no harm to gardens or crops because, unlike chickens, they don't scratch the ground. Their agitation upon sighting dogs, foxes, or hawks can save the lives of other, less diligent poultry.

Farmed pigeons are particularly promising as urban micro-livestock because they require little space, thrive in cities, and forage over a very wide area. Dovecoats are a good source of garden manure and meat; young pigeons (21 to 30 days old) are called squab, and yield a finely textured meat.

Although they require a pen because they don't stay close to home like other poultry, quail produce a staggering number of eggs, and their meat is extremely low in fat and cholesterol. (Turkeys raised as free-ranging foragers likewise produce a very low-fat meat.)

Many species of wild birds in the rainforests of Latin America such as chachalcas, guans, curassows, tinamous, and trumpeters could be domesticated or ranched within the forest itself. These birds could make much-threatened forest land more valuable than land destroyed by felling trees for cow pastures. Finally, the potential of Megapodes, the eggs of which are widely gathered in Papua New Guniea and Indonesia, should be further researched.

Rodents

Although raising rabbits takes more time and skill than raising chickens or other scavengers, they are especially well adapted to households in which capital and fodder resources are limited, and they can do much to improve the diet of needy families. In theory, a single male and four females can produce as many as 3,000 offspring a year, representing some 1,450 kg of meat—far more than one could get from a cow. Rabbits have more protein and less fat and calories per gram than beef, pork, lamb, or chicken. In view of this, many countries are promoting small scale pro-dution through advertising and school education programs. The long-haired Angora yields a luxury fiber, as much as 1 kg per rabbit. The fur and leather of the more familiar breeds can likewise become a valuable source of income. Rabbit manure is an excellent fertilizer, containing high amounts of nitrogen, phosphorous, and potash, and is often marketed in convenient dry pellet form. Unlike poultry manure, rabbit droppings need not be composted and can be immediately dug into the soil.

Rodents are eaten in many countries. They are so popular, in fact, that many have become extinct, while others are on the verge of becoming so. Indians of the Caribbean ate a number of indigenous rodents, one the size of a bear, causing several to become extinct just before the time of Columbus. The cloud rat of the Phillipines, the mara of Argentina, the vizchaca of South America, and the hutias of the Caribbean have all been hunted to the verge of extinction. The domestication of non-endangered species is already underway, with the raising of capybara in Venezuela, paca in Panama, the giant rat in Nigeria, and the grasscutter in Ghana. Because of their invasive potential, many of these rodents should not be farmed outside their native range.

Non-native rodents can become true pests, as in New Zealand, where opposums were introduced into an environment with no predators, and indeed no mammals. At present, the opposums are destroying New Zealand's forests by eating the greens off of trees. The challenge in such a case is finding a way to usefully control the number of such animals, probably by some combination of predator introduction and farming/ranching. Another rodent which has become a pest is the North American grey squirrel, introduced into Europe; the challenge is finding ways to turn such "pests" into economic and ecological advantages.

The recently rediscovered "thinking rat" of the Solomon Islands (one of six rodents once widely eaten but now presumed to be extinct), the kiore of Polynesia and New Zealand, the bamboo rat of Sumatra, and the giant New Guinea rat could all prove to be valuable food sources. Finally, the familiar pet guinea pig is perhaps the ultimate user-friendly microlivestock. It is quiet, odor free, and allowed to run loose in thousands of dwellings in the Andes, where it has been raised and eaten for centuries. The low cost of guinea pigs makes them available even to landless peasants. Converting kitchen scraps into meat, 20 females and two males may produce enough meat year-round to provide an adequate meat diet for a family of six.

Microantelope and Microdeer

Although there is considerable experience, most notably in New Zealand, with rearing large species of (introduced—in the case of New Zealand) antelope and deer, their miniature counterparts, standing between 20 and 40 centimeters, represent a virtually unknown resource in some areas and are being hunted to extinction in others. In all cases, these animals are adaptable to the harshest conditions, provide excellent meat and pelt, eat forage that most other livestock find indigestible, and are resistant to many of the diseases to which livestock such as cattle are susceptible. The muntjac, a native of Asia, has become wild in England and, unlike many other alien species, is an asset rather than a nuisance to native plants and trees. The pudu, brocket, and huemul are the three little-known types of South American microdeer; with the exception of the huemul, they could provide a valuable economic resource.

Small antelope called duikers are an extremely popular food throughout much of Africa, from the densest rainforest to the driest savanna. Many species thrive in the savanna, rainforests, and secondary forests, and through illegal hunting are already making a significant contribution to the African larder. Over-hunting of the once-abundant duikers, however, is leading to a significant decline in their numbers. Africa contains large expanses of uninhabited land which do not produce any kind of commercial livestock; these would be idea places to introduce microlivestock such as duikers.

Microantelope are widely hunted and eaten throughout Asia and Africa, and are currently being eliminated over broad areas of their ranges; turning them into a sustainable and economical food source would provide strong movivation for their conservation. The best long-term solution for many species of wild microantelope and deer is thus to organize their husbandry through forest ranching, herding, or farming, depending upon the proclivities of the animal in question.

Large Lizards and Iguanas

Lizards have been an important human food since prehistoric times, and are still commonly hunted in parts of Asia, Africa, Latin American, and Australia. Iguanas offer promise as microlivestock because their meat is popular throughout much of Latin America (fetching higher prices than pork or beef), and they do not compete for food, feeding on leaves, flowers, and fruits that are too high in the trees to be gathered by humans or livestock. As with microantelope and small rodents, indiscriminate hunting and habitat destruction is leading to a worrying decline in their numbers. Pilot studies in Panama and Costa Rica show that these animals are easily farmed at the forest edge; once reared in captivity, they tend to stay near where they were raised if simple wooden shelters are provided. The sustainable exploitation of iguana would be a viable alternative to cutting down forests for farming or cattle rearing; raising iguanas could thus conserve tropical forest while providing people with meat and income.

Bees

These insects are so common as microlivestock that little needs to be said about their potential, other than that they are uniquely suited to urban food production. The practice of rotating hives in farmers' fields can greatly improve agricultural productivity by increasing pollination rates.

Miscellaneous Microlivestock

Often eaten by indigenous peoples, animals such as worms, edible insects, frogs, turtles, and bats could reap the benefit of natural habitat protection while providing the Western world with new, nutritional food sources, if we dropped our cultural taboos against consuming them. In Thailand, for example, where community forest land is being cut down to provide space for eucalyptus plantations (which damage the soil and deprive the villagers not only of valuable vegetables, fruit, and edible leaves, but also of the frogs, ant eggs, beetles, and crickets upon which they depend for nourishment during the dry season), great use is made of these nontraditional animal food sources:

> Silkworms, grasshoppers, ants' eggs, tadpoles—the list of edibles that nature offers to northeastern peasants is endless. In the hot season, when fish are rare and ponds have turned into puddles, villagers spend most of their days in the fields or nearby forests looking for food. January is relatively kind to us as there are still fish in the swamp, and we can always find clams, water snails, tadpoles, and different sorts of frogs nearby. The tadpoles are usually prepared with chile into a spicy northeastern laab, mixed with fermented fish or wrapped in banana leaves and roasted. Frogs are at their best in an om, sharing the bowl with ground rice, chili, and any available vegetables. But tadpoles and frogs have become increasingly rare because of the use of batteries to catch fish. They electrocute the fish, but kill off frogs and tadpoles as well. As for the birds, they return in February and stay until May, but there have gradually been fewer birds over the years as the forests have disappeared. With the March heat, villagers have to turn to looking for ground lizards, edible insects, and beetles. If there is a brief shower of rain during this time, we set out in hordes looking for jeenoon beetles. They come out to eat the sprouting leaves. All we have to do is light fires under the trees and they just fall off onto the ground. In May, apart from grasshoppers and crickets, red ants and ants' eggs are the delicacies of the month. Expert eyes will not miss an ants' nest hidden in a mass of wilted leaves, glued together like a basket. When the nest is shaken with a long stick, worker ants and their eggs fall out and are caught in a bucket of water, but the hunter-gatherer dashes away in a flash to escape being bitten by them.[1]

In Australia, although kangaroo and emu meat are now being made "legal" and becoming more culturally acceptable among whites as food, many smaller animals such as native lizards, snakes, and turtles are protected on conservation grounds from being hunted or consumed. The commercial farming of larger animals such as crocodiles and water buffalo has done much to conserve species and protect the environment. There is no reason why these principles should not be applied to smaller animals. Many of the smaller wallabies, now on the verge of extinction, were once widely consumed by aboriginal peoples. The fencing off of land from feral cats, as well as intensive breeding programs, could provide both economic and conservation reasons for preserving Australia's indigenous microlivestock.

Finally, giant clams can each produce over one million eggs at a time. Recent attempts to repopulate reefs in northern Queensland with them were so successful that the navy had to be called in to shift the surplus youngsters to more remote reefs. Clams are capable of delivering a staggering 18 tons of high protein meat per hectare (a hectare equals 2.471 acres). Instead of genetically engineering larger and larger sheep and cattle, and killing millions of kangaroos in order to provide grass for such large domesticated livestock, Australians might be far better off looking at their own indigenous food sources and learning that small, indeed, may be truly beautiful.

Meat or Wheat?

Both medical and environmental science show us that the large scale production and consumption of beef, pork, and mutton is unhealthy and unsustainable. But the simple switch from meat to wheat (however valid from an ethical point of view) is not in itself very likely to do much to improve the fertility of the soil, conserve wilderness, or increase food production. Paddy fields release as much methane as do cows, and the large-scale monocultural production of rice is little better for the environment than the large-scale monocultural production of sheep and cattle; both practices simplify ecosystems and discourage diversity by focusing upon an extremely narrow range of domesticated plants and animals.

Humanity must learn to use wilderness and marginal lands effectively, and stop using them for large-scale livestock rearing and monocultural agriculture. Enriched land polyculture, in which edible and nutritious native fruits and tubers are encouraged, together with the free-range ranching of native wild species, represents by far the most ecologically rational approach to the use of land in terms of both food production and the conservation of wilderness diversity. Edible native fruits (many of which have a much higher vitamin content than conventional ones) should be encouraged through enriched land polyculture, and gathered along with native animals in times of high rainfall and seasonal abundance. Even in Europe, the potential for enriched polyculture is very great. During World War II the shortage of imported fruits in England led people to collect rose hips, which are very high in vitamin C, from hedgerows. Lesser celandine is another very common wayside flower which is remarkably high in vitamin C; it was once collected to be taken on ships to prevent scurvy. Scores of different types of nuts, fungi, fruits, leaves, bulbs, and berries, many of which are highly nutritious and consumed by a great variety of animals, were once collected from European and American woodlands. If the cultivation or protection of edible plants could be encouraged as part of the reforestation and revegetation of meadow lands, this would not only provide food for game animals and birds, but wholesome meat and fruits for us as well.

Excluding animal husbandry from food production oversimplifies the ecosystem and ignores the co-evolution of plant and animal life. In almost any region, modified forms of animal husbandry can coexist with fruit, grain, and vegetable production. The intelligent combination of these, in small-scale, integrated, and well-managed animal/plant systems, is often the only effective way to increase soil fertility and eliminate the use of harmful chemicals used for pest and weed control. Many animals consume feeds that cannot be eaten by humans; and the growing of these animal foods does not conflict with vegetable and fruit production. In many cases, animals can be used to target insects and weeds which inhibit agricultural success. Animal manure is a necessary part of any stable ecosystem; clearly, the range of useful products that can be obtained from animals is not restricted to the meat which they produce.

To insist upon the ethical correctness of vegetarianism or veganism is one thing; to claim that such practices, if universally adopted, would automatically improve the environment and increase food production is misleading. Large scale production of a very few breeds of very large meat-producing animals, fed upon monoculturally produced grassland, grain, or fodder, is a sickly product of industrial capitalism. Cutting down rainforest to grow grass to feed cattle to make hamburgers for consumers in rich countries is absurd and destructive, but there are a thousand ways to produce meat, grains, fruit, and vegetables in harmony with one another, at the same time enhancing the health of the land and soil upon which we all depend. It is thus not meat-eating *per se*, but the large scale monoproduction of both animals and grains (especially those that are fit for human consumption) that is the ecological culprit.

---

1. *Behind the Smile: Voices of Thailand,* by Sansitsuda Ekachai. Bangkok: Thai Development Support Committee, 1991, pp. 41-43.

Wilderness and
The Human Community

Will we allow our children to stare in awe at a free eagle hovering over a beautiful, unspoiled mountainside? Or will we only allow them a last-chance glance at a few miserable specimens in wire cages? What is the anarchist vision for the health and continuing evolution of life on Earth in wilderness areas; and what of the species that such areas sustain?

The French anarchist/geographer Elisee Reclus, writing over a century ago, clearly saw the need to preserve the great wilderness areas of the Earth from obliteration by industrial capitalism. The preservation and expansion of wilderness was necessary if humanity was not to fall into decline. The "wilderness experience" was, for Reclus, an essential part of childhood; without it, adults' appreciation of life would be stunted:

> Those who traverse the Pyrenees, the Alps, or the Himalayas, or even the high cliffs along the seashore, those who plunge into the depths of the virgin forest or look down into a volcanic crater, learn, while looking at these magnificent sights, how to appreciate the true beauty of less striking scenery, and when they have the power of modifying it they will not fail to respect its peculiar features. We must therefore wish every success to that noble passion which impels so many men, and, we must add, the best among men, to penetrate into virgin forests, to traverse seashores and mountain gorges, and to examine nature in all the regions of the globe where she has preserved her primitive beauty. It is now felt that, unless we wish to subside into intellectual and moral weakness, it is necessary that the vulgarity of so many ugly and commonplace things, in which narrow-minded people think that they discern the evidence of modern civilization, should be counterbalanced at any cost by the contemplation of the

magnificent scenery of the earth. It is necessary that the direct study of nature and the consideration of its phenomena should become one of the principal elements of education for every cultivated man; . . .[1]

Although Reclus goes on to talk of "beautifying the surface of the Earth and . . . making it that pleasant garden, dreamt of by the poets of all the ages," a careful reading of his work reveals that he was not calling for the creation of a carefully bio-engineered planet in which the Earth's wilderness is transformed into a tame utopia. He was calling for, rather, a world which held forests enough for encounters with Blake's "tyger," but which also held a place for civilization's gently rolling gardens and fields, a place for both Shelley's "skylark" and Hopkins' "brinded cow."

But today, many assert that human civilization is incompatible with a clean environment, and some extreme critics assert that human civilization is inevitably *lethal* to the environment. Do we face a choice between the free and spontaneous evolution of wilderness life or the manipulation and partial (or complete) destruction of our birthplace? Must we allow the biosphere to remain unfettered by human purpose and design, or must we turn the wilderness into a giant garden, engineered to our own requirements? While either choice is infinitely preferable to destroying 99% of the Earth's biological inheritance in the name of capital and state, neither is a viable solution.

Two facts are obvious: first, the environment needs protection, especially where it is most threatened; second, humanity is just one among many millions of species living and evolving upon this planet. It is necessary to preserve those areas which have been left for the most part undisturbed by human agro-industrial activity. Without wilderness, life's ability to spontaneously evolve will be crippled, and we cannot allow this to happen.

The preservation and expansion of wilderness cannot be accomplished without fundamental changes in the civic life of humanity. We are burning the environmental candle at both ends—the city and developers' bulldozers at one end, cattle and barbed wire at the other.

We must cease regarding wilderness and rural areas as disposable economic resources. The idea that "backpackers' parks," wildlife refuges, and national parks (the latter usually located on land which was not considered financially viable for development) are adequate wilderness areas for the evolution of the Earth's many lifeforms strikes most environmentalists as biologically naive, if not downright ludicrous. Wilderness should lap at the fringes of our cities and towns—large native birds and animals should live right there, occasionally swooping down or wandering into our suburban gardens. Substantial areas of every ecological region need to be given over to wilderness, to the free and spontaneous evolution of the biosphere—and not just to humans and their pathetic handful of domestic animals and plants. This entails not just "conserving" small "pockets," but actively expanding the amount of wilderness in each ecological region. In many areas, this will probably involve the removal of unnecessary roads and inappropriate satellite suburbs as part of the purposeful deconstruction and reconstruction of our urban and rural space.

But the reconstruction of urban and rural life according to ecological guidelines cannot be ethically accomplished via dictates from above. People cannot be forceably removed from their houses or deprived of their roads and local services by governmental forces, as the Pol Pot regime did in Cambodia with horrifying results. The grand work of reconstruction can only be accomplished through concerted education and increased awareness of the goal of cooperative bio-regional communities. Practical interim solutions include the establishment of wildlife corridors between existing nature reserves and, more practically, the enhancement of "buffer zones" around existing parks in order to preserve their central and ancient cores. In time, even these minimal steps would produce significant areas of wilderness in every ecological region on Earth.

Predators

Until recently, predators such as tigers, sharks, bears, and wolves were viewed as humankind's enemies. The dramatically dangerous and ferocious beasts of the adventure story were tracked down and shot wherever they were found. Since the advent of the stone axe and the flint-tipped spear, however, such animals have ceased being much of a threat to human populations. Nevertheless, a fear of predators has given force to the irrational wish to tame and destroy the wilderness that shelters them.

Fortunately, a more rational approach that combines fear and respect for wildlife is emerging. (Of course, we should not be naive about how dangerous wildlife really is.) Australia's attitude toward the crocodile and the shark is at last moving away from a "shoot and kill" mentality to one of respect and curiosity. Since the commercial hunting of crocodile stopped (at the brink of extinction) in Australia's Northern Territory many years ago, people have gradually come to respect crocodile warning signs by waterholes and have learned to swim where it is safe. On Queensland's Gold Coast, enthusiasts are at this very moment capturing and then moving sharks from an inland canal system and returning them to the ocean, instead of indiscriminately killing them every time someone is hurt or killed.

Europe—A Land Without Wilderness

In most of Europe, wilderness preservation does not even present itself as an issue. In Great Britain, for example, the battle is not over wilderness but over ancient woodlands and meadows. The wilderness disappeared there 2,000 years ago, and 95% of all the original wetlands have been drained. In England, the last wolf was killed around 1600, and several thousand years before that the mammoth and the bear disappeared. The Scottish highlands still have room enough for a few bears and wolves, and the reconstruction of wilderness might, in some cases, allow the reintroduction of some of these animals into England. The wilderness ethic currently so fashionable within some Australian and American radical environmental circles has little meaning, then, for Western Europeans, with the possible exception of those living on the Iberian Peninsula.

Restoration of Wilderness

In advocating the restoration of the wilderness, we should be careful not to reject the capacity for rational human behaviors. Some extreme conservationists believe that it would be in our species' and our planet's interest to prevent all human access to existing national parks and wilderness areas. Those holding this belief ignore the value of positive, rational human intervention. Prior to European colonization, for example, the Australian aborigines managed extensive areas of wilderness and helped preserve thousands of species of small marsupials through selectively burning the bush. The cessation of rational aboriginal land management with the advent of European settlement was a large factor in the early extinction of many small marsupials. In many areas of the globe, humanity will have to consciously intervene in order to ensure the preservation of wilderness—and this work more often than not will necessarily involve large numbers of people. The attempt to prevent access to wilderness through authoritarian controls is uncalled for and unworkable. Humanity cannot and must not be cut off from nature.

Even that which we now denote as wilderness has in most cases been manipulated and transformed by the activities of our ancestors, and as long as humanity remains on this planet, the fate of wilderness areas (as well as our own) is intimately dependent upon how we individually and collectively relate to them. Inactivity is not a serious option on a living and constantly evolving planet. Those parts of the world designated as wilderness must be expanded, not placed off limits to all but a handful of park officials. However, current human activities within wilderness areas, from crass tourism to vastly inappropriate techno-fixes (such as the New Zealand Park Authority's sprinkling of vast tracts of native bush with insecticide pellets that they presume only possums will eat) are clearly misdirected. Rather, the people of an ecological region must work together to ensure the restoration of its natural ecosystems. Restoration will be slow, arduous, and labor intensive—let no ecocrat persuade you otherwise. Free from the stress of capitalist overproduction and of needless forms of labor, workers more often than not will have the time to enjoy clean air and forests while simultaneously engaging in activities that lead to the expansion and renewal of essential natural resources.

The Oceans and Atmosphere

The boundary between land and sea is not simply a "fence" between different regions; it constitutes, rather, an ecosystem, in fact a form of wilderness, in its own right. In some places the shallows stretch for miles out to sea, with mangrove swamps covering huge areas of the world's coastline. Coral reefs, island chains, bays, inlets, and deltas make for unique coastal environments in which the distinction between land and sea becomes almost meaningless. Whole classes of plants and animals are especially adapted to these areas, where life enjoys the rich habitats accorded by the mixing of land and water. It is the province of seals, gulls, crabs—and humans. The presence of land and ocean together creates, as it were, a doubling of the potential for life. Indeed, the beach is where all terrestrial life began, as creatures moved from sea to land many hundreds of millions of years ago.

Nonetheless, for many people the ocean represents a completely alien world. Although humans have always prospered and evolved on the world's beaches, beyond coastal waters the ocean becomes a place of danger, where humans, unless safely aboard some vessel, are ill-equipped to survive more than a few hours. Our fear of drowning and of the unknown has for centuries led us to invent ghastly sea monsters capable of devouring a ship in a matter of seconds. Until the submarine and the underwater camera, exactly what lay at the bottom of the ocean was more of a mystery to our species than what lies in outer space—at least one can see the stars! Novelists, dreamers, and visionaries of the past imagined huge undersea cities built upon the ocean floor, much as modern science fiction depicts alien civilizations upon marvelous planets in distant galaxies. The deep sea creatures recently filmed by underwater photographers appear as alien to us as any space monsters dreamed up by the film industry. Thus, although the boundary between Earth and space is indeed "the final frontier," the border between land and sea is undoubtedly the last frontier that exists here on Earth.

Oceanography and marine ecology are showing us that the oceans are not simply great expanses of water, but that they consist of a diverse group of oceanographic regions. Among other factors, volcanic activity, peculiar currents, and vast differences in depth, fertility, and temperature have compounded to make a patchwork of distinct aquatic regions and subregions every bit as diverse as the terrestrial ones with which we are familiar.

The fact that so many of the Earth's bioregions are un-inhabitable (for our species) offers some problems for social anarchists. The bioregional approach to the environmental crisis is quite rightly dependent upon the notion of "re-inhabiting" one's region—the argument is that only if people identify deeply with the regions in which they live will global bioregional harmony be attainable. The question arises, how is such harmony to be achieved when so little of the Earth's surface is or has been inhabitable for us?

The largest unihabitable land area is Antarctica, which has recently become the subject of international debate. Although the world's governmental leaders eventually decided to adopt a "wait and see" policy toward the proposed mining and "economic development" of the Earth's last great terrestrial wilderness, they dismissed out of hand the inherently reasonable idea put forward by Greenpeace that Antarctica be declared a "world park." Antarctica's adjoining ice sheets in some ways make it a midpoint between land and ocean, and though it has never had a resident human population, it is a haven for much of the world's best-loved marine life. It is unfortunately, however, one of the most fragile environments on our planet. Antarctica needs humans like Australia needs rabbits, and the idea that humanity should consider it a global park is an eminently sound proposal.

I believe that if we are going to achieve global environmental harmony, it is necessary to extend Greenpeace's proposal for Antarctica to include all the Earth's great oceans. We should designate all the oceans as world parks—over which no individual or human nation can lay any legitimate claim whatsoever, and in which we have absolutely no right to interfere. This is not an extreme position; the extent of the damage that humanity has inflicted upon the world's oceans in rendering whole classes of marine life near extinction has yet to be properly addressed. The world's oceans, rather than being the province of nuclear submarines, driftnets, and oil tankers, must become a new sphere of human social and ecological cooperation. The forthcoming global federation of terrestrial bioregions must begin its work by declaring the oceans world aquatic reserves, whose ecological integrity must be preserved.

Although we cannot "inhabit" ocean regions, our perception of and interaction with oceans must change from one of indifference and brute exploitation to one of care and respect. At present we barely understand the enormous potential, dynamic complexity, and immense regional diversity of the vast expanses of water we call oceans. Instead of regarding the oceans as irritating obstacles to human movement—expanses of water to be crossed or ruthlessly harvested for food—we are at last beginning to overcome the "frontier mentality" of pillage and waste, and starting to think constructively and responsibly about the Earth's aquatic inheritance. Rather than regarding blue whales as hundreds of tons of floating meat, we are instead taking our first tentative steps toward communication with these mighty creatures. The dolphins that play with people at Monkey Mia on Western Australia's coast show us that our efforts to cooperate and communicate with marine life are likely to be both rewarding and reciprocal.

The quest for wilderness preservation and global ecological harmony does not end with respecting the oceans. They may be the "final frontier" on Earth, but there remains an even less-explored frontier—that of the atmosphere between Earth and space. Like all boundaries in nature, the atmosphere is not a simple, clear-cut boundary; rather, it is composed of many layers, all of which play vital and complementary life-preserving functions. Like the oceans, the health, stability, and purity of the atmosphere is essential to planetary homeostasis. In turn, both land and sea are profoundly affected by the slightest change in the composition of gasses in the atmosphere, as can be seen in the emerging and horrifying details about the greenhouse effect and ozone depletion. Clearly, not only must the terrestrial federation of bioregions make peace with Earth's aquatic regions, but together they must make peace with the atmosphere.

Although the clouds, tree tops, and mountain summits in some senses represent the boundary between the biological and non-biological, like all things in nature they are deeply inter-dependent. It is in promoting the harmonious *interactions* among the terrestrial, aquatic, and aerial regions of the Earth—both wilderness and nonwilderness regions—that we will restore the health and vigor of the global organism.

---

1. *La Terre*, by Elisee Reclus, translated by B. Woodward, 1873 .

Anarchism and Community Self-Defense

In the past, when people depended upon their local region for provision of their basic necessities, defense of that region was synonymous with self-defense. The need to protest and protect—not in the name of this or that "ism," but in order to save precious local ecosystems—is again emerging as a fundamental individual and community necessity. The fight to "save the earth" begins at home, where all can participate in local social and environmental reconstruction. Since it transcends ideology, this struggle can potentially unite young and old, women and men, black and white. This development joins community consciousness with self-determination.

The efforts of suburbanites to save a local park and the struggle of the native peoples of Sarawak to save their forests are both attempts by local inhabitants to assert control over their environments. Anarchists simply ask people to move beyond sporadic community actions and instead to assert the right to regional self-determination—leading ultimately to a global federation of eco-regionally integrated communities.

Self-defense is considered a fundamental individual right in our European democratic tradition. In a situation in which people have been intimately dependent upon the same forest for thousands of years, eco-defense becomes self-defense. Without the forests and kinspeople upon which they depend, indigenous people are individually defenseless. It is for these reasons that "natives," armed only with arrows or spears, defend their territory to the death. Europeans, by contrast, are stuck like flies in a spider web—paralyzed little individualists confined in little brick boxes, feeling powerless to protect the environment around us from despoliation.

It is only when local people come together to defend their environment against the excesses of corporate greed that change can come about. Since it has been promoting the ideal of local self-determination for more than two centuries, anarchism contains the seeds of the contempory Green idea of eco-defense. Not only does it assert the absolute right of people to defend their locality from external interference, it also encourages like-minded people in various communities and regions to federate with one another to set up their own nongovernmental and non-capitalist forms of organization.

But in the megalopolis, where the majority of people now live, the population has long since been uprooted from the native lands of its forebears; city dwellers no longer even dream of engaging in protracted land-based campaigns against occupying armies. Modern city dwellers feel lucky if they own their own houses or trade tools; and they can no longer fall back upon an intimate knowledge of the terrain for collective self-defense—the loss of a formidable skill, even in these days of military satellites and heat-seeking missiles.

Uprooted from their native soils and all too frequently alienated from the ecology of the surrounding countryside, the people of the city can become helpless victims of military aggression. Crouching like rats in cellars and subway stations, their only salvation is "media attention" and help from outside. In the past, before the development of the nation state, when towns were independent, the city defended itself as a city, defined by its encircling defensive walls. Its citizens were intimately acquainted with the ecology and rural lifestyles of the surrounding country-side, and rural people looked to the city for protection from military adventurers, rogue kings, and other scoundrels. But today, the walls of the medieval city of Dubrovnik are just so many useless old stones in the ethnic violence currently plaguing the Balkans nation states.

Military Madness

The modern military has the capability to launch an all-out attack upon the environment any time it chooses to do so. It need no longer limit itself to fighting other armies, or to massacring civilians; rather, it can destroy the organic and in-organic infrastructure of an entire region—leaving the region's people (along with the plants and animals) hapless victims, like sea birds in an oil slick. The most famous recent example is that of Saddam Hussein, a man driven insane by the corrupting influence of near-absolute military power, who attempted to destroy the ecology of the Kuwaiti desert by blowing up its many oil wells.

In South Vietnam, the U.S. military, through chemical defoliation of vast tracts of forest, attempted to destroy the ecology of an entire biological region in its pursuit of military victory. This attempt to defoliate and toxify an entire forest ecosystem was unprecedented. The defoliation of huge areas of Vietnam's forests was, to the megalomaniacal U.S. government, like selectively weed-killing a small corner of communist nettles behind the backyard shed. Realizing that the long-term results of military campaigns on foreign terrain are far from certain, the U.S. military invested in the development of weapons of mass destruction which would not only destroy "the people" in one decisive attack, but would also destroy their environment for generations to come.

Capitalist Madness

Such occurrences are almost trivial compared to the routine, unceasing destruction of nature under state-sponsored capitalism. Loggers cut trees 24 hours a day in some forests of Southeast Asia, using enormous mobile spotlights at night. Thus, when the military arm of the state-capitalist order is not destroying regional ecologies, the anti-social, profit-at-any-price economic arm of capitalism is doing the same thing, but more slowly. Anarchists oppose both the military state and the capitalist system, advocating the development of regional and interregional eco-defense networks.

Eco-defense differs from both military offense and defense; its thrust is essentially peaceful and preemptive. The eco-defense of a region involves peaceful, regenerative, and constructive activities, the aim of which is to defend the beauty and natural ecology of neighborhood and bioregion. These activities include the establishment of local seed banks to preserve rare and threatened species, the regeneration of native bush lands, and other such benign behaviors. Local skills exchange networks, Green action alliances, and a host of other Green organizations all practice eco-defense.

At some point, however, force will be met by force; the state is never afraid to use the police and the army to impose its will against the wishes of people in revolt. Eco-defense implies attacking the state/capitalist system from within as well as from without. While it is workers who actually build the bulldozers and machines of war, they/we ultimately have the least to gain from the resulting damage. From a capitalist standpoint, workers are the weakest link in the chain of the military-industrial complex. Greens, workers, and Green workers must join together to collectively defend the ecology (and ultimately the economy) of the regions in which they work and live. One urgent task facing eco-anarchists is to convince our fellow workers that preservation of the environment is in their/our best economic interests. A good example of such an effort is the current IWW/Earth First! educational and organizing campaign among timber industry workers in Northern California.

The Role of the State

For centuries, nation states have forcibly relocated people when they deemed such removal necessary to their interests. Examples range from the movement of entire nations by Stalin in the early 20th century Soviet empire, to the British declaration of Terra Nulla in conquered lands (that is, aboriginals did not exist or were not human, and were rather a "lower" species of hominid!) The flesh and blood results of such deliberate dislocations are people crammed into labor camps, missions, and refugee stations—deprived of their land and tools, or dragged as children from their parents in order to be taught to be good little citizens.

Throughout its history, the state has attempted to eradicate regional differences and de-territorialize entire nations, reducing everyone to cogs in a huge, colorless, eventually industrial megamachine. And this de-territorialization of the people by the state is becoming more complete every day. The aim is to produce an urbanized robot with no organic connection to the land upon which s/he lives. A human who is little more than a social security number adrift in a sea of social anomie is incapable of effectively resisting the amassed power of capital and state.

The government knows that people must be taught to displace their inborn sense of connection to their kin and their home region. Indoctrination of nationalist beliefs and identities is therefore one of the main purposes of compulsory state education —to teach people that they are French rather than Breton or Basque, and English rather than Cornish or a Northcumberlander. In England, the destruction of regional languages through the enforced teaching of Latin or the Queen's English buttressed the Act of Enclosure (confiscation by the state of the English "common lands"). Forced from the high meadows of Cumberland to work in the cotton mills of Lancashire, the uprooted and exploited suffered the double humiliation of working 14 hours a day for paltry wages and of watching their children perish from malnutrition and disease. In response to this situation—and with the spectre of the Paris Commune before its eyes—the English state saw fit in the Education Act of 1871 to mandate that all children under its control go to school, where they would learn that they were "English" and must curtsey to the Queen. The Basques, Bretons, Catalans, and Welsh peoples were, for modern European states, unwelcome reminders of the dynamic pre-Roman regionalist order. The languages and cultures of these peoples have been either directly outlawed or indirectly destroyed through compulsory (mis)education and saturation-level exposure to mass media.

Despite the sad legacy of hundreds of years of Roman imperialism, the Welsh, Basques, and Bretons survived, and it is their dogged ability to resist state military and cultural conquest which is of real interest here. Social anarchists argue that such strong regionalist sentiments should now be taken out of the context of petty nationalism and transferred to a non-nationalist, universal concept of self-defense of one's local region from state encroachment. The fight of native peoples throughout the newly industrializing world is only the front line in the historic battle against the uprooting of humanity by statism/capitalism. While we must do what we can to assist indigenous people around the world, we must also strengthen the rearguard, defending the regional integrity of such home places as remain in the "developed" world.

Eco-Offense

All anarchists desire an end to war, but anarcho-pacifists insist upon strict adherence to pacifism, in order not to contaminate peaceful ends with the violent means that some argue will be required to overthrow large, centralized military states. Some anarchists thus reject eco-offensive behavior (that is, acts that may involve destruction or sabotage, though with no threat to human life or limb). This nonviolent approach shows a commitment to peace, and is morally defensible.

Some eco-offensive actions undertaken by organizations such as Greenpeace—especially those involving courageous, nondestructive stunts—have proven remarkably effective in winning over large cross-sections of the community to greener ways of thinking. This may be partly due to the fact that the real targets of Greenpeace's actions are the mass media, not the whalers in the next boat. A century ago, an altercation between two boats at sea would have been the basis for some drunken sailor's yarn. But everybody in the world today is able to enjoy real-life drama on the high seas from the comfort of their own living room. The media are indeed a circus, and a modern-day "pirate" story is simply too much for them to resist; Greenpeace's nonviolent eco-offensive stunts are as much global media events as were the environmental destruction of the Kuwaiti desert in the Gulf War, and the Exxon Valdez disaster in Alaska.

Sabotage

Beyond publicity stunts and imaginative but essentially peaceful protests, we must consider the subject of sabotage. Eco-sabotage involves the deactivation of bulldozers, the blocking of logging roads, etc., in an effort to slow down the depradations of the state/corporate machine and to remind workers in harmful occupations that others in their community do not approve of their activities. On the surface, sabotage appears to be more offensive than defensive, but the seemingly offensive nature of commando-type attacks on environmentally dangerous industries can be justified as defense of the Earth. The aim of the eco-offensive is not military gain or individual profit, but rather the general defense of wilderness and nature for the benefit of all.

Sometimes, however, sabotage turns nasty and violence results—almost always initiated by representatives of the state or corporations. Most people are aware of the eco-destruction being wrought all around them, and largely understand the basic difference between acting in one's own interest and acting for the good of the planet. They generally, and quite rightly, regard saboteurs as idealists, not as common criminals or vandals. The long jail terms meted out to the Vancouver Five by the Canadian government, the bombing of the Rainbow Warrior by the French secret service, the car bombing of IWW/Earth First! activists Judi Bari and Darryl Cherney by timber company goons, and the entrapment of Earth First! founder Dave Foreman by the FBI, coupled with the entrapment and imprisonment of four of his colleagues, all clearly testify to the fact that, when it feels threatened, the state/capitalist order employs all means—fair or foul, legal or illegal—against its "enemy."

Whatever philosophical problems we may have with justifying attacks upon environmentally ruinous projects, those qualms do not alter the fact that state/capitalist enterprises seriously damage the processes of life and are therefore profoundly unethical. The perpetrators of environmental outrages have the support of police, armies, prisons, and the advantage of superior communication systems—a colossal arsenal of organized military violence. It is not my place to say whether the eco-defensive campaign to "Save the Earth" should involve large-scale engagements with the forces of state and capital. War is war, an all-out opposition of force by force; it usually occurs when all possibility of peaceful reconciliation has vanished, when resolution can only take place (or so it seems) through the victory of one side or the other. Anarchists have always hoped that consciousness building and dialogue among the workers of the world would result in organization of worldwide opposition to the production of arms, thereby averting the possibility of more violence and war. Unfortunately, this has not happened. In both World Wars I and II, workers were happy to produce armaments for the state in an international orgy of nationalistic slaughter. The critical question is whether humanity will become aware of the life potential of a peaceful federation of nonhierarchical eco-communities soon enough to avoid more widescale violence.

Timber Wars

Perhaps the most important current example of eco-defense is the IWW/Earth First! campaign to save Northern California's redwoods. It's thus worthwhile to consider the lessons to be drawn from that campaign, and a good jumping off point is the recent book, *Timber Wars*, by IWW/Earth First! activist Judi Bari.

Judi Bari was born in the U.S. in 1949. She became a student activist during the Vietnam War years before dropping out of college. She worked as an industrial worker for the next 20 years, and became involved in the union movement. She helped to organize two strikes—one of 17,000 grocery clerks in the Maryland-D.C.-Virginia area, and the other a successful wildcat strike against the U.S. Postal Service at the Washington, D.C. Bulk Mail Center. In 1979 she moved to California, and a decade later became involved with Earth First! Teaming up with her friend Darryl Cherney, she began to organize opposition to the destruction of the few remaining pockets of ancient redwood forests in Northern California. After one assassination attempt and numerous death threats, Bari was nearly killed in a car bombing in 1990 that left her crippled for life. The FBI never seriously investigated the bombing; instead, they attempted to frame Judi and Darryl, claiming that they had been victims of their own bomb, an absurd and slanderous claim that was quickly discredited by available evidence.

The assassination attempt did not, however, stop the Redwood Summer eco-defense campaign that Bari had been organizing. Outrage over the bombing encouraged new people to become involved; and IWW/Earth First! actions and organizing campaigns continue in Bari's home area of Mendocino County to this day.

Redwoods and Rednecks

All is well neither for the once-mighty redwoods of California nor for timber industry workers; and things are unlikely to get much better in the near future. The timber industry has a policy of cutting every tree more than a foot thick, and redwoods do not even begin to seed until they are about 130 years old. The timber industry has brought in new machines which can literally pluck small trees out of the ground, and it's even hatched a plan to extract the few remaining 1000-year-old trees out of gorges with helicopters. The redwood ecosystem has now almost vanished. What will be left for the inhabitants of logging communities when the timber companies inevitably leave? The residents of these communities, although aware of their predicament, continue to scramble to remain wage slaves just a little bit longer.

If the loggers and mill workers had organized an effective union, they might have been able to insist on a sustainable harvesting plan. Sadly, this didn't happen—through no fault of Bari and her fellow organizers. The real losers in this battle were timber industry workers, who were simply unable to work in solidarity with one another. In the words of one of them:

> "The workers are up against the wall—but they're not organized. I've thought for years that there should be a timber workers union. It's hard because there's so many levels of employment. There's a guy out there working in the woods, there's a guy hauling logs to the mill, there's a lot involved. But without organization, well what good's it going to do me to quit when Joe Blow down the road is going to go ahead and take my job?"

In the past, the lumber companies employed immigrant crews "who were always afraid of having to go back to something worse," and whose strikes "were crushed with a level of violence that's hard even to comprehend." Radical unionism in timber country simply never re-established itself after being obliterated during the 1920s by the combined forces of capital and state. Lack of unions led to very bad wages and working conditions—timber workers lived in hell while they helped to destroy a paradise; but the prospect of immediate unemployment was even worse.

So, the timber companies know that the workers will submit to almost anything. The mills are run by mean, petty dictators who disregard industrial safety in order to meet production quotas, and conditions in the woods are no better. Loggers are often crushed or poisoned by chemicals:

> Logging is the most dangerous job in the U.S., according to the Labor Department. The death rate among loggers is 129 per 100,000 employees, compared with 37.5 for miners. . . . In 1986 the companies knowingly sprayed chemicals over an area where a logging crew was working, poisoning 12 to 15 people. The loggers' skin turned beet red, they had severe headaches, diarrhea and nausea, one man threw up blood and another man's wife had a miscarriage after handling his clothes. The company maintained that the loggers just had the flu . . . and threatened them with a lawsuit if they caused any more trouble.

If life is bad in the woods, it's just as bad in the mills:

> The work rules are designed to turn you into an automaton. . . . You have to be at your work station ready to go when the start-up whistle blows, or you can be written up for lateness. Three white slips in a year and you're fired. . . . Amid constant noise and visible sawdust in the air . . . whole logs run through a two-yard-tall band saw. The off-bearer stands a few feet from these saws and uses a hook to grab the slices of log. There are no guards on the sawblades, just exposed, high speed, spinning teeth. The off-bearer must wear a face shield to protect himself from flying knots or metal debris from the logs, but that's not always enough to prevent injury. Because the knots are few and far between, the bearer is not always alert. It can run cool for a week or a month, then wham!—something pulls the saw off.

Because they've generally failed to organize, loggers and mill-workers perform these terrible jobs for minimal wages. Constant speed ups and increased production quotas make the work increasingly dangerous. By contracting jobs out to old employees as private contractors, the timber companies further reduce the possiblity of industrial organization among workers. In the words of one equipment operator:

In the wintertime when logging was not going on my boss
subletted me and my piece of equipment to do some highway
work. I was getting $8.50 an hour to run my piece of equipment,
and there was an 18 year old girl that was standing there holding
the flag all day, and she was getting $22.50 an hour. [Why?] She
is in a union!"

The reasons for such miserable conditions are not that many
of the workers do not understand what's going on, nor that Bari
and other agitators did not try to get loggers to organize to save
their jobs and the environment. Rather, abhorrent conditions pit
workers against each other over jobs, and local law enforcement
agencies make sure that attempts to unionize loggers are ruthlessly suppressed. As well, the timber companies and AFL-CIO
bureaucrats have persuaded most loggers to despise and distrust
environmentalists through a deliberate misinformation campaign.
Pages and pages of Bari's book expose news blackouts, press lies,
and FBI double dealing. The Klu Klux Klan, the U.S. Army,
vigilante committees, and right-wing religious nuts are just some
of those who have joined together to prevent Earth First! from
trying to halt ecocide. Who bombed Judi Bari remains a mystery,
but there is certainly no shortage of criminals who could have
carried out the attack. Harassment, intimidation, threats, misinformation, corruption and complicity were all blended with pre-
meditated physical violence to destroy the perceived ringleaders
of the environmental movement. Even a 15-year-old boy who
invited Bari to talk at his school received death threats.

The role of alternative media in publicizing such things, Bari
concludes, is vital:

If an Earth First! demo happens in the forest and nobody writes
about it, did it really exist? . . . When you look as bad as the
timber industry, only a complete news blackout can help public
opinion. It's not surprising that an industry that would use
assassination to suppress dissent would also use censorship. We
can't depend on the corporate media to publicize our battles with
the corporations. That's why newspapers . . . are so important.

Eventually, the determination of Earth First! and the growing
realization among timber workers that their jobs were doomed

(due to corporate logging practices) led to Judi Bari's gaining some respect in logging communities. This was not due to chance, but to continuing efforts by Bari and other IWW/Earth First! organizers. She organized an IWW union local in Fort Bragg with both timber workers and Earth First!ers as members. She also officially represented five timber workers at an industrial tribunal after PCBs were dumped on them at work. (Both the timber company and the workers' sell-out AFL-CIO union tried to cover up the spill by saying that it was just mineral oil.)

A Few Lessons

Had timber workers formed truly independent unions, eco-catastrophe could have been avoided and logging regions might have been able to develop a sustainable resource base. Un-fortunately, most of the workers that did organize, organized against Earth First! and took part in their own industrial suicide. This tragic lack of communication between Greens and workers is also a feature of current timber wars in Australia, where union "leaders" (as in the U.S.A.) continue to tell workers that environmentalists will take their jobs from them. To combat this, we must encourage the formation of anarcho-syndicalist unions that will expose these lies and ensure the implementation of genuinely sustainable forestry practices. Bari pinpoints tame business unionism and the lack of industrial syndicalism as the most important factors in the environmental battle:

> What is needed is some direction, and it's certainly not coming from the AFL unions. Earth First! is still leading the battle in the woods, but Earth First! can only do so much because it is not a workers' organization. Historically, it was the IWW who broke the stranglehold of the timber barons on the loggers and millworkers in the nineteen teens. The ruling class fought back with brutality, and eventually crushed the IWW, settling instead for the more cooperative business unions. Now the companies are back in total control, only this time they're taking down not only the workers but the Earth as well. This, to me, is what the IWW-EarthFirst! link is really about.

Bari also subjects Earth First! as an organization to a great deal of criticism. She admits that her "relationship with Earth First!, outside 'Ecotopia' [an autonomous EF! affinity group], has always been strained at best." A large portion of *Timber Wars* criticizes EF!'s co-founder, Dave Foreman, and the lack of understanding of labor issues within the organization. Foreman and Ed Abbey built up a highly individualistic, EF! mountain man image, exemplified in Abbey's influential novel, *The Monkey Wrench Gang*. It depicts eco-saboteurs within the context of a conventional adventure novel which reads much like a survivalist tract.

Foreman has always portrayed himself as a patriot and has claimed that "anarchists and class-struggle leftists have infiltrated EF! and led it away from its true purpose." Bari quotes extensively from Foreman's book, *Confessions of an Eco-Warrior*, and is deeply critical of his reactionary social vision:

> He proudly calls himself a patriot and a Republican. His heroes, mentioned repeatedly in his book, include white-man land rapers like Washington, Jefferson, and John Adams instead of biocentrists like Chief Seattle or Vandana Sheeva. . . . 'Most people in this country,' he says, 'myself included, respect the concept of private property.' Well, wait a minute. If you really believe that nature is not here to serve humans, and humans are merely part of nature, how can you support the idea that humans can 'own' the Earth? . . . Foreman's middle class bias is also shown in his contempt for industrial workers: 'We are inconsistent when we castigate [a timber baron] for destroying the last wilderness redwood forest, yet feel sympathy for the loggers working for him,' he says. . . . Now, I don't hold any romantic views about the noble proletariat . . . [but] it seems to me that people's complicity should be measured more by the amount of control they have over the conditions of their lives than how dirty they get at work.

Bari denies, however, that Earth First! has become a traditional leftist organization, and she presents us with a vision similar to the social anarchism of Elisee Reclus, but which is instead inspired by the modern biocentric philosophy of deep ecology:

> It is wrong for Dave Foreman to characterize us simply as leftists or a class struggle group. . . . [Socialist] theories deal only with how to redistribute the spoils of exploiting the earth to benefit a

different class of humans. We need to build a society that is not based on the exploitation of the Earth at all—a society whose goal is to achieve a stable state with nature for the benefit of all species.

Green Feminism

Bari is as much a Green feminist as she is a Green syndicalist. In her critique of members of the Earth First! old guard, she displays both social perspectives. She is convinced that Ed Abbey was not sensitive to women's issues and bluntly states that his "retrogressive view of women as sex objects doesn't make it" in the newly feminized Earth First! And she unequivocally dismisses the *Earth First!* journal: "I'm absolutely clear that I've had it with the macho, beer-drinking, privileged bullshit it represents."

Judi Bari is also an ardent proponent of abortion rights, and religious nuts and misogynist anti-environmentalists have sent her innumerable death threats and hate letters both before and after the car bombing. The assassination attempt on Bari, a woman with two children, drew a lot more women into the Redwood Summer protests than there might otherwise have been. After the attack on her, Bari states that at least 20 people assumed vital leadership positions, three-fourths of whom were women: "This is the feminization of EF! Redwood Summer is an almost entirely women-led action."

The necessity of organizing in both the community and the workplace is basic to the theory of social anarchism; and the involvement of large numbers of women in the eco-defense movement, claims Bari, led to greater Earth First! involvement in logging communities. Isolated forest actions, in the absence of dialogue with progressive loggers, were therefore a tactical error on the part of the wider EF! movement:

> Earth First! was founded by five men, and its principal spokes-people have all been male. As in all such groups, there have always been competent women doing real work behind the scenes. But they have been virtually invisible behind the public EF! persona of 'big man goes into big wilderness to save big trees.' . . . For years the strategy of EF!, under male leadership, had been based on individual acts of daring. 'Nomadic Action Teams' of maybe 10

people would travel to remote areas and bury themselves in logging roads, chain themselves to heavy equipment, or sit in trees. There were certainly brave and principled women who engaged in these actions . . . but by and large, most of the people who had the freedom for that kind of travel and risk-taking were men. . . . I have nothing against individual acts of daring, but the flaw in this strategy is the failure to engage in long-term community-based organizing. There is no way that a few isolated individuals, no matter how brave, can bring about the massive social change necessary to save the planet. So we began to organize with local people, planning our logging blockades around issues that had local community support. We also began to build alliances with progressive timber workers based on our common interests against the big corporations. As our successes grew, more women and more people with families and roots in the community began calling themselves Earth First!ers in our area.

The Question of Nonviolence

Given the need for community support, the issue of non-violence was critical to the success or failure of Redwood Summer. Nonviolence, however, works best when those in power obey the law (consider the Tienanmen Square massacre), and Bari admits that this was a real problem:

Nobody ever said law enforcement in Mendo County was fair or logical. The problem is though, that sometimes these situations can be deadly. . . . We need equal protection of the law in this highly volatile struggle. We're nonviolent, but [we're] not going to go away and let the trees go down. . . . As our exposure and influence grew, so did the use of violence to repress us. And in this far-flung, rural, timber-dependent area, it was easy to get away with. At one demonstration an angry logger punched a 50-year-old nonviolent woman so hard that she was knocked cold and her nose was broken. In another incident, my car was rammed from behind Karen Silkwood style by the same logging truck that we had blockaded less than 24 hours earlier. My car was totaled and my children and I and the other Earth First!ers who were riding with us ended up in the hospital. In both these cases, as in other incidents of violence against us, local police refused to arrest, prosecute, or even investigate our assaulters. Earth First! had never initiated any violence throughout all of this. But neither did we publicly associate our movement with an overt nonviolence code. After all, that would contradict the he-man image that EF! was founded upon. Yet I did not see how we could face the increasingly volatile situation on the front lines without declaring and enforcing our nonviolence.

Bari is very certain about where she stands on terrorist violence. If you had nearly been killed and were left crippled for life by an act of terrorism, you too would certainly have strong views on the subject. Given what she has gone through, Bari deserves to be heard. She understands that nonviolence can in certain instances be unrealistic and ineffective. But she insists that terrorism of the sort directed against her is totally unacceptable:

> I had a discussion with somebody a week before the bombing and I told him that I considered nonviolence to be the only appropriate tactic in our country at this time, but that I considered it only a tactic. I wasn't a Ghandian who considered nonviolence to be the only way ever. I would never tell a Salvadoran to use nonviolence only. And he replied with an answer that has played out in my mind a thousand times since then. He said, 'Your belief in nonviolence as a tactic only will not sustain you through the hatred you're going to experience this summer.' I realize that I forgave the person who ran me off the road with the logging truck last summer in that he was victim who took his anger out on the wrong person. I could see that about him. They hauled him out of his truck and made him confront me, and I could see that he was horrified at what he had done. When he saw that my children were in the car too, he kept saying, 'the children, the children, I didn't see the children.' But the person who bombed me was a monster. I've been unable to understand how somebody would deliberately, coldly and premeditatedly try to kill me knowing that I have small children and I'm their sole support. And what I realized about myself . . . is that if you gave me the same bomb I don't have it in me to do it back to him. What I have discovered is that there's a level of violence, there's a level of terrorism that's really unacceptable to me. . . . I think that the problem isn't just the economic system, isn't just the social relations, I think that part of the problem is the violence in the society.

Nonviolence may indeed by the most appropriate way to defend a vulnerable Earth from a violent society. But what kind of society do we wish to create in its place? And what specific conclusions can we draw from the "Timber Wars"? The first is that successful eco-defense *must* be community based. Heroic individual acts are not in themselves sufficient to stop environmental degradation, and may in fact, in the absence of community support, (further) alienate local people. The second lesson is that workplace organization is the most effective community base for eco-defense. Bari realized this and, before the car bombing, was working to organize timber workers as well as to organize eco-defensive actions for the Redwood Summer campaign. The timber companies also realized the importance of worker organizing in eco-defense—which is almost certainly why they attempted to murder Judi Bari.

No one can read the future. Anarchists merely point out their ideals, defending their integrity of vision while fervently hoping that as little blood as possible will be shed in the coming social and ecological revolution. Thousands of anarchists have met untimely and horrible ends at the hands of state/capitalist jailors merely for expressing verbal opposition. Anarchists are not naive about the possibility of the absolute military or corporate/technological destruction of the entire human project, the destruction of our species. They appreciate the fact that once the battle between nature and the people on the one hand, and capital and state on the other, is raging, all of us will necessarily be forced to take sides, and perhaps to take up arms as well—though under present circumstances, at least in the industrialized world, taking up arms would be inappropriate, ineffective, and likely to do far more harm than good. (See *You Can't Blow Up a Social Relationship*, by anonymous Australian anarchists, and published by See Sharp Press, for further discussion of the political use of violence.) Peace, however, may become only an ideal, and not a realistic option, in an ecological "war." This "war" has already begun, and both sides are preparing for a battle between life and death upon planet Earth.

Anarchist Society
& Its
Practical Realization

The Historical Failure of Marxist Communism

The recent political and social changes in Eastern Europe have shown us that the marxist experiment with centrally imposed, authoritarian state socialism has been a tragic failure in both economic and human terms. Even persons who are hardened and relatively indifferent to the general welfare have been disgusted by the corruption, bankruptcy and sheer moral rottenness of the dictatorial state-communist system.

That the era of marxist "communism" has ended is beyond dispute. The people of East Germany literally voted with their feet. Lured by the promise of jobs, department stores, Sony TVs and Mercedes cars, they crossed the border to the West at a phenomenal rate. Separated by a wall of ignorance for so many years, the peoples of the former eastern bloc were naively convinced that the limited freedoms offered by western-style liberal democracy would somehow solve the many problems they faced. As they've since learned, nothing could have been further from the truth. As we approach a new millennium, we are surrounded by a multitude of seemingly incurable social and environmental problems—global in nature—which capitalism and parliamentary democracy are unable to solve. Beyond this, the so-called liberal democratic state, newly equipped with terrifyingly efficient methods of centralized social and information management, can be but a fragile guarantee of freedom and continued progress for the broad masses of people.

Despite the internal disintegration of international communism, coupled with the emergence of a "grass roots" and overtly radical ecology movement (which owes little or nothing to marxist ideology), a significant sector of the organized left appears unable to reject a narrow, outdated, mechanistic marxism. The "communist" states produced ecological destruction much worse than that in the western capitalist states, and certainly failed to guarantee human liberty and self-determination. If we are to convince people of the desirability of non-exploitative, non-capitalist social relationships, we must develop a language and a program that draws upon socialist traditions other than those of marxist communism. Social anarchism is prominent among these alternative traditions of revolutionary social organization and reconstruction.

Anarchism as an organized political force holds as its ideal the attainment of a rationally conceived, ecologically harmonious, non-exploitative and non-capitalist social system. Anarchism, however, unlike all other progressive political, social, and economic philosophies, regards the state in all its forms as an inherently corrupt, hierarchical, authoritarian and unworkably bureaucratic mode of social control that is incompatible with, indeed inimical to, the practical realization of a sane, just, and ecologically integrated society. Social anarchists, unlike marxist communists, do not seek to impose socialist concepts upon the people from above by means of centralized state structures. They hope, rather, that the people, in an attempt to produce a self-managed, directly democratic, and ecologically sustainable social system, will organize themselves from the bottom upwards—at the level of individual communities, interest groups, and workers' organizations.

Whether or not you agree with anarchists in believing that genuine social change in the direction of a socialist-ecological society can only come about with the destruction of centralized bureaucratic mismanagement, it is abundantly evident that the marxist attempt to impose socialism from above has been a tragic failure. The marxist-communist concept of the "dictatorship of the proletariat" or "workers' state" has always been realized as the absolute dictatorship of the Communist Party—that is, dictatorship pure and simple. *This is a very well proven historical fact.*

The Place of the Nation State in Social Evolution

According to archeological and anthropological evidence, humans have never lived as isolated, solitary beings. There were, of course, always outcasts and hermits who preferred or were forced to live alone; such people, however, have been the exception rather than the rule (like the rogue elephant or the lone dolphin). Humans, like so many animals (from elephants to monkeys), have evolved into socially complex and intensely sexual beings. Partly from the needs of survival and partly from the need to feel the touch of other kindred living beings, the human species has socially co-evolved in the most intimate fashion. Empirical evidence from the study of monkeys and apes assures us that our species was social before it was human. Thus, government as such is a quite recent social invention. History shows us that humans have lived for tens of thousands of years without feeling the least need for government. The nation state is thus an astoundingly recent social-evolutionary event. Any [Australian] aboriginal will affirm that this is so.

As the creationist mythology has been superseded by the theory of evolution, we have become aware that we are the product of a bio-evolutionary process in which nothing is permanent and everything is in a state of flux. As with biological evolution, the development of society (social evolution) has been a process of continuous adaptation, r/evolution and modification. The Stone Age, the Agricultural Revolution, the Bronze Age, the Industrial Revolution, the Communications Revolution, and the Reproductive Revolution are all stages in a dynamic and ever-changing social-evolutionary process.

As conscious beings, we can choose our collective social-evolutionary destiny. As a species we collectively engineered our social and political institutions, so it stands to reason that representative government and the nation state represent only one of many possible modes of social organization.

We as a species constructed the institutions of government and state, and likewise we can dismantle them. We can replace them with better forms of social organization, forms that do not rely upon constituted authority and large and inefficient centralized bureaucracies. Evolution is an ever-open book, and the nation state, which has been with us only a few thousand years, is but a small paragraph in a long and ever-changing story.

The future of our planet and our continued evolution are under grave threat. Important social r/evolutionary choices must be made. The nation state has not been particularly successful in solving the enormous social and environmental problems we face, nor have governments solved the problems of violence and war. (Indeed, until quite recently the Russian and American governments were threatening to blow one another up with nuclear missiles and probably destroy the entire ecosystem of our planet in the process.) Governments have consistently failed to preserve the integrity of our soils, rivers and forests. The imperialist empires of the last few centuries, for example—the most extensive form of state exploitation and domination yet known—inflicted irreparable environmental damage not merely upon particular ecological regions, but upon entire continents. The introduction of new animals ill suited to the prevailing ecology, and the exploitation of local bio-resources—fertile lands, forests, game, etc.—to provide raw materials for the short-term benefit of distant imperial states, has resulted in huge tracts of land being turned into pitiful deserts.

If humanity is to survive, we must stop blindly placing our faith in government. The continued evolution of our species can no longer be left in the hands of official bunglers. Only the people at the level of the individual household, factory, and community can initiate the social-ecological r/evolution. The state has always been a mechanism which supports the rich and powerful who, far from being interested in the future of our species and our planet, are interested only in their own wealth and self-aggrandizement.

A social and political organization lasts as long as the people are willing to abide it. Within reason, any social system, no matter how vicious, destructive or stupid (apartheid or Nazism, for example), is workable in the short term if enough people believe in it. But if enough people are convinced of the desirability of organizing society on a nongovernmental basis, then anarchism, as an organized social force, becomes a realizable social-evolutionary choice every bit as practical as centralized government and the nation state.

Anarchism, the State & the Technological Revolution

Most people are indoctrinated from the cradle to the grave to regard government as the source of all social order. Despite the many hours on television and the many pages in our newspapers devoted to political issues, the media has never deemed it interesting or relevant to ask the question: *Is Government Necessary?* Despite all the corruption, silly disputes, unnecessary secrecy, bureaucratic ineptness, and sheer dishonesty which have always accompanied parliamentary politicking, the media continually glorifies the state—producing an endless stream of overtly statist propaganda thinly veiled with a nauseating display of shallow patriotism (as during the 1991 Gulf War). Media representatives constantly hound government leaders and officials, pouncing like dogs at the dinner table upon every dropped word, and they fill their news and opinion columns with the dreary details of petty party intrigues.

People raised from birth to regard government as a natural and essential part of the social order are not surprisingly a bit bewildered when confronted with the idea of running our social and political affairs without it. "Surely," they object, "the abolition of government would result in the destruction of organized social life and simply result in chaos!?"

In fact, it wouldn't. Nongovernmental organization is a normal part of everyday social life. Whether government exists or not, people cannot help but develop complex patterns of social organization. For every human need or interest, you can guarantee that some form of social organization will spontaneously emerge in order to serve it—usually with no connection to government. Babysitting networks, trade unions, horticultural associations, hobby groups, volunteer fire departments, and the Red Cross are just a few examples from the multitude of voluntary social organizations which developed independently of government in order to serve social needs. Many of these spontaneously evolved social organizations remain local or last but a few weeks or months to meet the needs of the moment. Others assume a more permanent character, and some develop an international character. In fact, there is an enormous pool of nongovernmental forms of association and organization which could be developed to serve virtually every human need and interest. (Of course, voluntary organizations are not meeting all social needs at present, and almost certainly cannot do so while capitalism endures. This is due in large part to the grossly inequitable distribution of wealth and income in capitalist states, and to the truly staggering amounts of money siphoned off by governments.)

No single centralized national or international government can ever hope to consider, let alone adequately deal with, the immense diversity of human needs and concerns. A group of a few hundred people passing laws and resolutions on pig farming one day, reproductive technology the next, and public highways the day after, without any of the legislators ever having managed a pig farm, engaged in medical or reproductive research, or built a road, is, in our modern, complex society, simply an absurdity.

Social anarchism does not imply the absence of organization. Anarchists simply want to remove centralized governmental organization and coercive authority. Although anarchists will not accept the *irrational* authority of a handful of politicians (whose only expertise is in the acquisition of prestige and power), anarchists, like humanity's tribal ancestors, respect the *rational* authority of the expert. If one wishes to learn about wine making, one approaches the workers of the wine-making industries—and respects their expertise in matters of wine making.

Placed as we are at the advent of the technological, computer, and communications revolution, we need to forget childish conceptions of parliamentary government. They belong to a past era. For we are entering the information age—an age in which billions upon billions of bits of data concerning all things imaginable whiz hourly around our globe. A technological-communications revolution in which there is the cooperative interchange of views, information, and expertise in all areas of human interest, without the interference of government, will bring changes that we are only beginning to fully appreciate.

Instead of placing our faith in burdensome, inefficient, and overly centralized parliamentary bodies as we do at present, social anarchists urge that we create a society which is administered by a multitude of separate organizational bodies: education groups for the furtherance of study; environmental groups for the preservation and management of natural wilderness; organizations for the protection of human liberties and for the promotion of peace and arbitration; industrial workers unions representing every conceivable trade and industry; statistical accountancy associations for the management and rational allocation of scarce resources— all of which will work together in their particular fields of activity, both locally and globally, for a better, healthier, greener and more rationally self-administered society.

New technology has, however, also placed enormous and terrifyingly powerful tools in the hands of the state. Already the government is insanely attempting to administer society through massive central computers (e.g., Social Security, the IRS, etc.). The state, in its desire to centrally and hierarchically administer an incredibly large number of people in an ever more complex society, has had to resort to ever more sophisticated computers which place enormous quantities of information and power in the hands of fewer and fewer people. Huge and powerful computer banks (with information on everyone and with little or no public access) are not only inefficient in that they obviously fail to take into account the variety and complexity of human life, but dangerous in that the potential for misuse of their information on a vast scale by tyrannical political elites is simply terrifying.

Anarchists abhor this dangerous development and argue for the computer-assisted management of things rather than people. Anarchists maintain that the technological/communications revolution must be used for the benefit of all humankind. They want a free and openly communicating society in which a multitude of specialist organizations will federate and cooperate with one another for the realization of a better, self-administered society.

Big Brother or social anarchism—this is the choice which confronts us. We the people must decide the course of the social-technological r/evolution.

Anarchism, the State & the Social-Ecological Revolution

Environmentalism is at the forefront of current political and social debate. Even previously committed nature haters such as Margaret Thatcher have, in an effort to capture the Green vote, begun to give lip service to environmentalism. Politicians have begun to hug trees rather than babies at election time.

Government, however, will have no place in the forthcoming social-ecological revolution. Even now, under the threat of ecological disaster, it takes the bravado of a few committed environmentalists in nongovernmental and nonparty organizations such as Greenpeace to pressure the government to reluctantly enforce the few paltry regulations on the books.

When the masses of ordinary people have perceived the necessity of changing the course of social evolution, governments of all types have always proven inadequate. Even the most "progressive" of governments, because of their very structure, are capable only of dull, slow, and bureaucratically tortuous reformism. Placed as we are now at the brink of the social-ecological revolution, it is obvious that the governmental system will never be able to keep abreast with the demands of the people. The wholesale "greening" of nations cannot be accomplished by a few hundred politicians sitting in legislative halls.

The people, perceiving that government is incapable of fostering the great environmental and social changes needed to ensure their continued survival, must begin to form their own groups and organizations. People in their neighborhoods and suburbs should set up recycling depots and communal composting sites without waiting for government "approval." Workers, through their unions, should boycott the use or reckless disposal of dangerous substances and implement newer and safer techniques without waiting for the government to pass new "industrial regulations" or for their employers to change their ways. We must begin to organize ourselves without paying heed to what the government may or may not say. If we do, the fall of government and the nation state becomes inevitable.

As the social-ecological revolution progresses, people will begin to organize themselves not according to electoral and state boundaries, but rather according to natural geographical and ecological ones. Electoral and state boundaries, being artificial creations unrelated to naturally occurring boundaries, will be completely useless in the forthcoming social-ecological revolution. (When the English army invaded and colonized Australia it divided the country—more or less with a ruler and a pencil on a piece of paper—into six separate states. What impudence! What stupidity! To defy millions of years of evolution and draw a straight line through a desert or a forest and call this half Western Australia, this half the Northern Territory!)

The existence of a huge number of distinct and unique ecological regions and sub-regions with their own special mixtures of flora and fauna is something that the nation-state system, born of Caesarism and imperialist conquest, has largely failed to recognize. The people, anxious to protect the biological integrity of the region in which they live and bring up their families, rather than relying on the orders of some distant government, will themselves begin to repair the damage caused by reckless capitalist exploitation and by centuries of imperialism. The social-ecological revolution thus implies anarchy. For in the new age of ecological radicalism and biological realism, the political boundaries of the statist era will necessarily be replaced by natural, ecological ones.

This will not simply be a "retribalization" of humanity—for we can never return to a past age. Besides, the human species is at last beginning to think in global terms. "Think globally, act locally!" is the slogan of the 1990s. The need for clean air, and the intercontinental migration of bird and marine life, show us that the distinct ecological regions are not closed entities. The wellbeing of any ecological region, however unique or isolated (e.g., a South Pacific atoll), is dependent upon the wellbeing of all the others. One hopes that the people of each ecological region will quickly realize that in addition to striving to ensure their own wellbeing, they must also strive to take a responsible place in a complex, global federation of environmental forces.

The ecological-anarchist approach to global environmental problems is to save the whole by saving the parts. Social anarchists encourage people to stop relying upon government to solve their problems and to realize that they have much influence in their own neighborhoods. Eco-anarchists claim that the only rational approach to planetary bio-federation and environmental stability is to persuade people to deeply identify with the natural ecology of their local place and to protect that place while developing industrial and agricultural practices that are adapted to its ecological characteristics. If this were to happen in every natural region, argues the anarchist-ecologist, then the planet as a whole would be much better protected against the destructiveness of our present social system, and that system would almost certainly be replaced in short order.

A global federation of ecological regions will necessarily be nonhierarchical, for it is impossible to rank the value of one ecological region above another. Each may have an unforeseen and significant role to play in ensuring the long-term ecological stability of our planet. Yet, at present, some regions are relatively well protected while others are ruthlessly exploited. How can it be that the environment of Yellowstone Park is more important than that of a "national sacrifice area"? (The U.S. government has deliberately destroyed—mostly through its nuclear programs—a number of natural regions in pursuit of its "national security" interests. Government bureaucrats refer to these devastated regions as "national sacrifice areas.")

Clearly, government can have no part in the forthcoming social-ecological revolution.

Anarchism, Social Revolution & the Free City Commune

When anarchists speak of the destruction of the nation state, people often assume that they're advocating a return to small scale village or community life. Although anarchists would certainly like to see villages and towns become independent and self-governing, a return to a small scale, essentially isolated communal lifestyle on a mass scale is both repugnant and implausible. Anarchism is not a backward-looking, pre-industrial ideology. Even though the development of fast and efficient transport and communication systems has eliminated the need to live in larger and larger cities, when anarchists speak of the destruction of the state they are not promoting small, isolated communities.

What they are promoting is the destruction of empire-style organization; and there are assuredly empires within empires. Much as imperialism is the control of foreign lands by an alien and centralized entity, the nation state itself is a mini-empire. Each national government is situated like a spider in its web, ruling the most distant cities and townships from Canberra, Paris or Berlin. Is this a necessary or, indeed, even a practical way to organize society? Social anarchists argue that it is not necessary, and not even very practical, and that the primary, natural unit of social life ought to be the free, independent, self-governing city.

With the destruction of the nation state during the social revolution, the people themselves will begin to administer the affairs of their cities. Just as people are beginning to consider themselves inhabitants of distinct ecological regions, they will likewise come to consider themselves not as subjects of the nation state, but as equal citizens of a particular town or city. The people of each city, free of the torpor of centralized, bureaucratic mismanagement, will assume a new sense of civic responsibility. Rather than wait for directives from the capital or city hall, they will meet in their workplaces and neighborhoods to discuss the problems of the day and to decide what to do about them. The dismantling of state-centralism will initiate a flourishing of civic involvement such as has not been seen since the decline of the ancient Greek or the medieval European cities, when each city considered itself a sovereign entity—independent, self-governing, and answerable to no one. The citizens of the cities will no longer regard themselves as belonging to a particular state, but to a particular city with its unique history, traditions, trades, and architecture—a city situated, moreover, in a distinct ecological region which needs their vigilant care.

As the communal revolution progresses and the people of each city develop an ever-deepening sense of civic identity, the whole geography of the liberated city will begin to change. The city's districts and suburbs, instead of being powerless and centrally dominated units in an undifferentiated urban sprawl, will become independent and vital urban communities. In an effort to become self-sustaining and to prevent the degradation of the countryside, the city's people, in cooperation with rural people in the sur-rounding ecoregion, will dispense with outdated, environmentally unhealthy forms of monocultural agriculture and instead imple-ment local, organic, and community-based forms of agro-industrial production. The citizens of each urban district will themselves become responsible for meeting their municipal and civic needs—housing, health, settling local conflicts, entertain-ment, primary education, childcare, and a host of other things. Thus, social anarchists hope to replace the nation state with a large number of agro-industrial city communes, that is, an agglomeration of federated, yet independent, townships.

Despite inevitable conflicts between opposing factions and districts, the necessity of sustaining a sense of civic unity and purpose will ensure that for the most part disputes will be peacefully settled. A self-governing and sovereign city freed from external state interference must, as a matter of necessity, resolve its own problems. Everyone needs safe streets, shelter, food, entertainment and relative peace, so it is in the interests of every citizen to sustain an active, healthy city—a city which provides plentiful, high quality food, that is sustainably integrated with its surrounding bioregions, and whose architecture, landscaping, parks, and vitality provide sustenance and wonder.

This does not imply a return to the Dark Ages, when each city was surrounded by fortifications and essentially isolated. For this dates from a time when it took many days on horseback to travel from city to city. Fast and efficient transport and communications networks will never allow a return to that era. Of necessity, cities will federate with one another on the basis of culture, ecology, trade, industry, and location in order to secure information, goods, and services which are universally required but not readily available in particular cities or communes.

The forthcoming social anarchist revolution will be a communalist one—not a mere coup d'etat or the transfer of power to a new Caesar, general, or political party. The revolution will be decentralized and have thousands upon thousands of centers. The citizens of every city, town, and suburb will themselves set about reconstructing a pleasant, safe and ecologically sustainable civic community out of the ruins of the past state-capitalist era.

Anarchism, Social Revolution & Trade Unionism

Social anarchists, in both theory and practice, have always acknowledged the necessity of working class or trade union organization. However, when social anarchists talk about workers' organization, they do not speak in favor of the large-scale, centralized, and bureaucratic union structures of the present day. Such organizations are for the most part puppy dogs in the laps

of governments and corporations—"negotiating" in the most
servile fashion with our state-capitalist oppressors for the right to
remain wage slaves and to earn a couple more lousy bucks a day
(or, more recently, "negotiating" for our right to earn a couple
less lousy bucks a day). A centralized, bureaucratic trade union
organization whose entrenched, privileged leaders no longer
participate in the day-to-day work of the factory, farm or workshop, can never represent working people or even begin to
successfully utilize the immense social potential of grassroots
working class organization.

Obviously, this kind "unionism" has no place in any anarchist
society. For the workers in every farm, factory, workshop, or home
will have to take charge of production themselves. Engineers,
researchers, machine operators, apprentices, et al., will have to
cooperate among themselves, not for the benefit of a handful of
capitalists or state officials, but for the direct benefit of
themselves, their families, their industry, their city, and humanity
as a whole. Realizing that a particular plant or workshop cannot
organize an entire industry, the workers in each farm or factory
will federate with others in their trade in order to administer and
regulate their collective affairs. The trade union will, as a matter
of logic, cease being a bureaucratic, centralized body composed
of a mass of passive "members" controlled by a privileged hierarchy devoted to maintaining the employer/employee dictatorship—and their own privileged positions. The union will become,
rather, an organization composed of all the members of a
particular trade who will be collectively and publicly entrusted
with the proper functioning and development of *their* industry.

Individual trade unions will *directly* represent their workers
when discussing economic issues with unions in other industries.
They will be responsible to the general public—constantly inform-
ing the people of working conditions, trends, research developments, environmental safety, and other matters of interest. In
order to prevent the formation of permanent bureaucracies and
undemocratic procedures within these potentially all-powerful
economic organizations, anarchists stress several safeguards: the
democratic election of administrators by those they represent; the
rotation of administrative positions, with office holders returning
directly to the workforce after a predetermined period of time;

and, importantly, making everyone in administrative positions subject to immediate recall by those who elected them.

Working people, kept until now in servitude to capital and the state, are, in reality, the producers of *all* social wealth. All things essential to our day-to-day existence and continued survival—food, energy, transport, water, sanitation, etc.—are the products of human labor and natural resources which are (or should be) the heritage of all humankind. Once freed from working for the benefit of the few rather than the many, working people will quickly realize their true worth to society, which is cleverly hidden from them through a perverse social status hierarchy in which the rich—that is, those who live off the labor of others—have much higher status than those who perform useful work. (In fact, in our perverse society, the more useful the work, the lower its social status and pay seem to be—the jobs of garbage collector and childcare worker being cases in point.) Once freed from working to enrich the parasitic class, working people will soon acquire a new sense of independence, pride and self-worth, and their unions will serve both themselves and humanity.

The fact that trade unions are universal in character and not linked to a particular city or commune makes them ideal vehicles for a host of economically vital inter-communal activities. Anarchists believe that workers, through their unions, will ensure the equitable distribution of essential goods and services, some of which may be unobtainable at the level of the individual commune or city (e.g., coal and natural gas are found in only a few locations, but are required by people in almost all locations).

It is clear that if anarchists are to have any chance of realizing their goal of a stateless social order, then ordinary working people must develop nonbureaucratic and directly democratic forms of agro-industrial organization *in advance of the revolutionary moment,* capable of ensuring that vital services function efficiently in the absence of state-capitalist control. In order for the social-anarchist revolution to succeed, the trains, buses, mines, telephones, etc., must continue to operate from the moment the state-capitalist order begins to disintegrate. Without agro-industrial working class or trade union organization, revolutionary anarchism will remain an intellectual fantasy and philosophical pipe dream.

Anarchism & Revolution

Government will always be in permanent opposition to social evolutionary progress. In times of revolution, government will always attempt to stem the tide of social progress and will never keep abreast of popular demands. For government to do so would be contrary to its static, bureaucratic nature. Revolutions always involve the overthrow of the government of the day!

Having destroyed government in the revolutionary act, why then constitute another, as the marxists suggest? History has shown that attempts to create "workers' states" have always resulted in the development of vicious, totalitarian, bureaucratic police states. Revolution and government are incompatible—opposite and inimical to one another. The idea of a "revolutionary government" that will consolidate and further the revolutionary process is nonsensical. The reconstruction of government during the revolutionary process represents reaction and the end of revolution. We must break the cycle of governmental "revolutions" and embark upon the course of social revolutionary anarchism—the social construction of a rationally conceived, self-organized society in the absence of the nation state.

Revolution is a complex social phenomenon that is born of the people and which is a natural part of biological and social evolution. Centuries of oppression, injustice, and indoctrination have slowed the onset of revolution. But it will come. Through the long, dark centuries, there has been slow, painful progress; and it appears to be accelerating. Revolution is an accelerated social evolutionary process which involves the rapid modification or replacement of outdated social, political, economic, and ecological structures. Such transformations can never be the work of a single brain or of a scheme imposed from above through government. Revolutionary transformation involves the *whole* of society—not just a change of personnel in the controlling apparatus. A revolution must occur in every hamlet, village, town and province, however distant or remote. Revolution is the result of billions upon billions of revolutionary actions by millions upon millions of separate people, all of whom are striving, however vaguely, toward a new social order.

Revolution involves local action, the people in every street, park, suburb, farm, factory and workshop meeting to discuss events and to make collective decisions. It also involves direct physical actions such as the planting of trees, gardens, and fields, and the devising of new, nonpolluting and ecologically integrated ways of meeting humanity's many needs. The biosocial reintegration of humankind with nature and the development of genuinely democratic forms of political organization can only occur at the local level—at the level of each city and ecological region. Revolution, if it is to be successful, implies that millions of people take direct revolutionary action in their immediate locales, where only they can effect real and lasting political, economic, and ecological change. The immense social-ecological reconstruction of our planet can never be the result of dictatorship, bureaucratic reformism, or parliamentary politicking. It will be the social-r/evolutionary product of countless individuals, of humanity as a whole.

The nation state is a cumbersome and unnecessary leftover from an imperialist and profoundly anti-ecological era, capable only of supporting its own bureaucracies, multinational capitalist exploitation, and the privileges of the rich and powerful. Let us destroy the outdated monuments of the state-governmental period and through our unions, communities, and federations build a better, safer, greener, and more socially equitable world. Let us no longer place our faith in politicians who are only interested in dull reformism and self-aggrandizement, and place our faith instead in Anarchy—and in the ability of ordinary people to follow their own social evolutionary course and to construct a world capable of ensuring our species' continued survival.

The future of our planet is in our hands. We the people have the power to avert the social-ecological disaster that threatens us. To rely upon government—or god—is foolish and irresponsible. *There is no god, no "personal savior," no man on a white horse. Let us save ourselves!*

Bibliography

Abbey, Ed. *The Monkey Wrench Gang*. New York: Avon, 1976.

Bakunin, Michael. *God and the State*. New York: Dover, 1970.

Bari, Judi. *Timber Wars*. Monroe, Maine: Common Courage, 1994.

Berkman, Alexander. *The Bolshevik Myth*. London: Pluto Press, 1989.

    The Russian Tragedy. London: Phoenix Press, 1986.

    What Is Communist Anarchism? New York: Dover, 1972.

Bookchin, Murray. *The Limits of the City*. Montreal: Black Rose, 1986.

    The Modern Crisis. Philadelphia: New Society, 1986.

    The Philosophy of Social Ecology. Montreal: Black Rose Books, 1990.

    Post-Scarcity Anarchism. San Francisco: Ramparts Press, 1971.

    Toward an Ecological Society. Montreal: Black Rose Books, 1980.

Brinton, Maurice. *The Bolsheviks & Workers' Control*. London: Solidarity, 1970.

    The Irrational in Politics. Tucson, Arizona: See Sharp Press, 1993.

Bufe, Chaz. *Astrology: Fraud or Superstition?* San Francisco: See Sharp Press, 1987.

    The Heretic's Handbook of Quotations, Expanded Edition (editor). Tucson, Arizona: See Sharp Press, 1992.

    Listen Anarchist! Tucson, Arizona: See Sharp Press, 1992.

    "Primitive Thought." *Processed World* #22, 1988, pp. 16-17.

Collins, Joseph and Lappe, Frances Moore. *Food First*. New York: Ballantine, 1981.

Dolgoff, Sam (editor). *The Anarchist Collectives: Workers' Self-Management in the Spanish Revolution 1936-1939*. New York: Free Life Editions, 1974.

    Bakunin on Anarchy (editor). New York: Alfred A. Knopf, 1972.

Eichenbaum, V.M. (Voline). *The Unknown Revolution*. Detroit: Black & Red, 1974.

Ekachai, Sansitsuda. *Behind the Smile: Voices of Thailand*. Bangkok: Thai Development Support Committee, 1991.

Foreman, Dave. *Confessions of an Eco-Warrior*. New York: Crown, 1993.

Fourier, Charles. *The Utopian Vision of Charles Fourier: Selected Texts on Work, Love and Passionate Attraction*. London: Jonathan Cape, 1971.

Goldman, Emma. *Anarchism and Other Essays*. New York: Dover, 1969.

    Living My Life. New York: Dover, 1970.

    My Disillusionment in Russia. New York: Apollo Editions, 1970.

    The Traffic in Women and Other Essays on Feminism. Seattle: Times Change Press, 1970.

Goodman, Paul. *Utopian Essays and Practical Proposals*. New York: Vintage, n.d.

Goodman, Paul and Percival. *Communitas: Means of Livelihood and Ways of Life*. New York: Vintage, 1960.

Greco, Thomas H., Jr. *Money and Debt: A Solution to the Global Crisis.* Tucson, Arizona: Thomas H. Greco, 1990.

    New Money for Healthy Communities. Tucson, Arizona: Thomas H. Greco, 1994.

Griffin, John. *A Structured Anarchism.* London: Freedom Press, 1991.

Hayden, Dolores. *Redesigning the American Dream: The Future of Housing, Work, and Family Life.* New York: W.W. Norton & Co., 1986.

Hegel, Georg. *Phenomenology of Spirit.* New York: Oxford Univ. Press, 1977.

Ishill, Joseph (editor). *Elisee amd Elit Reclus: In Memoriam.*

Kropotkin, Peter. *Anarchism and Anarchist Communism.* London: Freedom Press, 1987.

    Anarchism: Its Philosophy and Ideal.

    The Conquest of Bread. Montreal: Black Rose Books, 1989.

    Fields, Factories & Workshops Tomorrow. New York: Harper & Row, 1974.

    Memoirs of a Revolutionist. Garden City, New York: Doubleday, 1962.

    Modern Science & Anarchism. New York: Gordon, 1980.

    Mutual Aid: A Factor in Evolution. London: Freedom Press, 1987.

    The Place of Anarchism in Socialistic Evolution.

    Revolutionary Studies. London: Freedom Press, 1892.

    The State: Its Historic Role. London: Freedom Press, 1987.

Leval, Gaston (editor). *Collectives in the Spanish Revolution.* London: Freedom Press, 1975.

Malatesta, Errico. *Anarchy* (Vernon Richards translator). London: Freedom Press, 1974.

    Life & Ideas (Vernon Richards editor and translator). London: Freedom Press, 1984.

Margulis, Lynn and Sagan, Dorian. *Microcosmos: Four Billion Years of Evolution from Our Microbian Ancestors.* New York: Touchstone, 1991.

Maximoff, G.P. *The Guillotine at Work.* Orkney: Cienfuegos Press, 1979.

Meltzer, Albert (editor). *A New World in our Hearts.* Sydney: Jura Press, 1978.

Michelle, Louise. *Memoirs.* University of Alabama Press, 1981.

Newman, James L. "Fertility in Transition." *Focus,* Spring 1986, pp. 4-5.

Orwell, George. *Homage to Catalonia.* London: Penguin, 1978.

Peirats, Jose. *Anarchists in the Spanish Revolution.* London: Freedom, 1975.

Prigoigine, Ilya. *Order Out of Chaos.* New York: Bantam, 1984.

Proudhon, P.J. *The Principle of Federation.* Ann Arbor, Michigan: Books On Demand, n.d.

Reclus, Elisee. *The Story of the Brook.*

    "On Vegetarianism"

    La Terre. (trans. B. Woodward) 1873.

Rocker, Rudolf. *Anarchism & Anarcho-Syndicalism.* London: Freedom Press, 1988.

    Anarcho-Syndicalism. London: Pluto Press, 1988.

Waldrop, M. Mitchell. *Complexity: The Emerging Science at the Edge of Order and Chaos.* New York: Simon & Schuster, 1992.

Ward, Colin. *Anarchy in Action.* New York: Harper & Row, 1973.

Wollstonecraft, Mary. *A Vindication of the Rights of Women.* New York: Viking Penguin, 1993.

(Anonymous). *You Can't Blow Up a Social Relationship.* San Francisco: See Sharp Press, 1990.